EVERYDAY Epiphany

Discovering God in Every Moment

EMILY HILL

WESTBOW
PRESS®
A DIVISION OF THOMAS NELSON
& ZONDERVAN

WestBow Press books may be ordered through booksellers or by contacting:

WestBow Press
A Division of Thomas Nelson & Zondervan
1663 Liberty Drive
Bloomington, IN 47403
www.westbowpress.com
844-714-3454

ISBN: 978-1-6642-9305-2 (sc)
ISBN: 978-1-6642-9307-6 (hc)
ISBN: 978-1-6642-9306-9 (e)

Library of Congress Control Number: 2023902997

Print information available on the last page.

WestBow Press rev. date: 03/13/2023

A WORD TO THE READER

If you're anything like me, you have probably started a devotional or kept a journal at various points in life. Sometimes it's the start of a new year, a response to boredom, an attempt at self-care, or just a time of change in need of documentation or guidance. Maybe one of those reasons led you to pick up this book, or maybe it was something completely different. But whatever brought you here, please know that you are welcome in this space!

There is no set structure to this devotional study. Move at your own pace. Pick it up and lay it down on whatever days and seasons work for you. This book isn't about checking off days on a calendar or reaching a set goal. It's about discovering God in the world around you. The world you walk through and participate in daily. It's about asking questions and recognizing God's voice when He responds. It's about learning who He is and connecting with Him beyond the church building. So grab a cup of coffee, a bowl of ice cream, or a glass of wine, and find a place to cozy up where you can take a step back and discover who God is and what He has been up to in your life.

EVERYDAY EPIPHANY

Every nativity scene usually has three guys holding gifts. We're not actually sure how many there were, but we do know that they were from out of town and had followed a star. Back in the day, the world was anticipating some sort of Messiah. They all had different ideas of who this guy would be, but everyone expected someone to show up and save them from the perils of this world. So when this bright star popped up in the sky, a group of wise and wandering men hit the sand and traveled toward the light. They believed that it was leading somewhere important and were willing to go on an unknown journey to discover what, or who, that might be. Traveling by the light of a star isn't the most direct route, but that didn't stop them.

They made a pit stop in Jerusalem, encountering King Herod and quickly realizing he wasn't someone they needed as a traveling companion. They were looking for a king, just not that one.

Back on the well-lit path, they navigated their way to Bethlehem. We're told that when entering the home and seeing Jesus, they fell and worshipped Him. In the church world, when we talk about these men and their gifts, we call it Epiphany. We call it this because it refers to their sudden realization of who that baby truly was and all that He meant for the world. But this kind of experience isn't limited to wise men in a desert following a star.

If you look up the word *epiphany* in a Google search, you'll find that it describes something simple and striking that is an illuminating discovery or realization. So what does that mean for us and God?

While we don't have a tangible light to follow in the sky like the wise men did, we can still follow the light. As we follow Him through the pages of scripture, we start to notice ways that word shows up in the everyday moments of life, guiding us closer to God amid challenges and changes. We find ourselves experiencing those simple and striking moments of epiphany, being introduced to the multifaceted character of God in our everyday lives.

> A Creator who doesn't make mistakes.
> A Healer who reaches the deepest wounds.
> A Guide who pursues and leads.
> A Provider who withholds nothing that is needed.
> A Comforter who weeps and knows our sorrows.
> A Savior who offers grace as a loving embrace.

Even if you have been following Jesus for a long time, I believe there is always still a journey ahead, leading to new discoveries and deeper levels of relationship. If you haven't met Him yet and this is a new adventure for you, my prayer is that you are simply willing to start this journey—even if it's with a bit of hesitancy—and seek the Light, wherever He might lead you.

A CREATOR WHO DOESN'T MAKE MISTAKES

"In the beginning …"

If you have never read the Bible, those words are a great place to start. If you have grown up learning about the days of creation, I invite you to open your Bible and check out this passage again. Genesis 1–2 details the events of creation and the work of our Creator. We are told that the voice of God formed the world when there was nothing but intense darkness. He projected light, separated the sky and sea, and spread out the dry land. Think about that for a second. There was literally nothing before He spoke it into existence. There was literally nothing until His voice illuminated the world.

But He didn't stop there.

After setting apart landscapes, He filled them with plants, animals, and people. As if simply creating the world from nothing wasn't amazing enough, He created a world that could endlessly grow and multiply in beautiful and remarkable ways. He created a world that was meant to expand and transform. He created a world that was alive and ever changing.

But He didn't stop there.

Fast-forward almost four thousand years, and you'll learn about a baby who was born in a tiny stable relatively unknown to the world. The angels proclaimed His arrival, and He grew in knowledge and grace, teaching as a child and performing miracles as a man. This baby was Jesus, who then went to the cross out of an abundant love for His creation. In a moment, He conquered the grave in a way that created a new path for the transforming power shown in the beginning.

The events of creation were the beginning of a passionate love story written by a Creator who breathed into life a world of beauty and continual renewal. The events of the cross show us the continuous grace of a Savior who breathed eternal life into His creation for a complete renewal.

The most incredible part is that this pattern of creation and transformation continues endlessly! With each baby born, there is a moment of creation and a lifetime of beautiful transformations. We grow and change from the time we are knit together inside our mothers' wombs until we breathe out our final breaths.

We are told in Psalm 139 that we are created, formed, and wonderfully made. It's a beautiful depiction of who God is and the tender loving care He uses to create His children. But as one of those children, I must admit there are times when it's really easy to pick out my imperfections, those that are seen by everyone and the ones I keep buried deep. Between my thick thighs and my less than loving thoughts, it's easy to feel like I'm falling short and struggling to keep it all together most days. On those days, I can't help but wonder, *Is this really how God created me?*

If you've ever asked that question, I'd like to help answer it for all of us as we discuss our Creator, journey in the garden with Adam and Eve, and discover evidence of who He is in our lives. I'll share with you some of my insecurities and stumbles with the hope that you will do the same as we seek to embrace ourselves as beautiful creations and honor our Creator.

Created in the Image of God

*So God created mankind in his own image,
in the image of God he created them,
male and female he created them.*
—GENESIS 1:27 NIV

WHO DO YOU LOOK LIKE?

Growing up, I often joked that I'm basically my dad without the beard. Although the joke stings a bit on those mornings when I pluck a couple of extra chin hairs before heading out the door, it's impossible to ignore that we are similar in appearance and personality. Our hearts are drawn to similar passions, and our tempers are enraged by similar frustrations. It makes sense. He is my dad after all. So if I am that incredibly similar to my earthly father, how much more am I like the One who actually created me, my heavenly Father? How much more should I be like Him?

The first book of the Bible says that we were all created in the image of God. Why? Because God was creating a world filled with His clones? No way!

We are created in His image so that we can be visible and tangible representations of who God is and what He's all about. Sin has distorted the image a bit over the years, with our thoughts and actions essentially disfiguring us. But Paul writes in a letter to the church of Corinth that we are able to be fully transformed into God's image, describing the experience as being similar to looking in a mirror.

> So all of us who have had that veil removed can see and reflect the glory of the Lord. And the Lord—who is the Spirit—makes us more and more like him as we are changed into his glorious image. (2 Corinthians 3:18 NLT)

That's hard for me to accept because I don't personally love mirrors most days. When gazing at my reflection, it is way too easy to pick out the blemishes, bumps, and bulges that I wish were different. But

Paul isn't talking about our outward appearances. We weren't created in God's image physically; it's deeper than that. When we focus our attention on God and invite the Spirit to transform us inwardly, we can then stand face-to-face with God, like standing in front of the most perfect mirror.

It's not like one of those mirrors that makes you look like you instantly lost ten pounds. It's actually way better than that. Our reflections become visions of Him in our actions, words, thoughts, and feelings. Our hearts become drawn to similar passions, and our tempers become enraged by similar frustrations. We truly become the image of God. We still have blemishes, bumps, and bulges on the outside because we don't lose our human flesh. But when we reflect the true image of God, we are transformed in ways that are seen, felt, and understood by everyone we meet.

We reflect the goodness of God beyond the mirror and carry His image with us and into the world.

Connection and Conversation

Standing face-to-face with God sounds like a simple idea, but it's actually something really incredible that was only made possible through the resurrection of Jesus and presence of the Spirit. To better understand what is so unique about the experience of standing face-to-face with God, let's go back and explore the ways Moses encountered Him. God and Moses had a relationship with open communication. They spoke to each other often, but there were specific times when God revealed Himself to Moses in more tangible ways. Read the following verses and write down some notes, focusing on how God interacted with Moses, his actions during the encounter, and the ways he was impacted following those interactions:

- Moses at the burning bush—Exodus 3–4
- A cloud of smoke—Exodus 19
- Moses on Mount Sinai—Exodus 24:9–18; 32:7–20
- The tent of meeting—Exodus 33:7–11
- The glory of God—Exodus 33:12–23; 34:1–9, 29–35

After returning with the tablets, for the second time, Moses was literally radiant from having been so close to the glory of God. But if you were paying attention, he didn't even really stand face-to-face with God. He was hidden in the cleft of a rock because God's glory was too powerful. Even so, his face was shining so brightly that a veil was required to cover it so that others weren't blinded by the light radiating from him.

Moses gathered everyone to give them instructions on building a portable tabernacle so they could have a place to worship on their continuing journey in the wilderness. They followed God's instructions to build a box designed to inhabit the presence of God, calling it the ark of the covenant. They also crafted a tent with a designated area for this ark and separated it from the people with a veil. This was a required separation from the presence of God. It sounds harsh to us because we've never had to live that way. But it was for the protection of the people. The presence of God was too powerful, and they would be consumed by the fire of His glory if they were too close.

Fast-forward to Jesus. Read John 14.

He was meeting with the disciples and told them He would be leaving soon. We know that He was talking about going to the cross, but this was all new information for His friends. To help explain the importance of everything being said, He says something kind of shocking. He tells them, "If you have seen me, you have seen the Father."

See why that was such a big deal? This was a group of guys who had grown up being told about Moses's shining face and a tabernacle separating the people from God so they didn't literally burst into flames. But now they are sitting face-to-face with someone who is saying they are actually looking at God by looking at Him now. And they aren't bursting into flames!

The disciples didn't fully understand what He was saying. But then Jesus actually goes to the cross. We're told that the veil of the temple was torn in two from top to bottom as Jesus let out His final breath. God's holiness didn't change in that moment, but our access to Him did. Jesus fulfilled what He spoke about and created a direct pathway to God.

The veil is no longer required because a new kind of closeness is now desired and accessible.

Remember that whole concern with bursting into flames when experiencing the holiness of God's presence? Well, after Jesus resurrected from the grave and ascended into heaven, His followers were gathered in a room when a rush of wind blew through, and flames appeared on their heads as they were filled with the Spirit of God. But they didn't ignite; they glowed like the burning bush that called out to Moses. Can you just pause for a second and really imagine how incredible that would have been to witness?

The flames eventually dissipated, but the Spirit remained within them. While we don't have the exciting appearance of flames, we are promised the same Spirit to dwell with us. God literally lives within us. How exciting is that?

We don't have to stand in front of a burning bush or behind a veil. We experience the presence of God within us when we receive Him in faith and reflect His glory around us as we share that with others.

DO WE LAUGH BECAUSE JESUS LAUGHED?

One of my kids asked this question a few years ago while trying to figure out what it meant to be created in God's image. It reminds me of a picture my grandma had that showed Jesus looking into the distance and laughing. But as I think about this silly and simple question from a child, I can't help but pause and think a little bit more seriously about the similarities I really should be sharing with the Son of God.

I was created in God's image, given His grace through Christ, and am guided by His Spirit. But does it always look like that? I make a lot of decisions and do a lot of things on a daily basis, but admittedly, I don't always look or sound much like Him.

> Someone cuts me off in traffic, and I have given a one finger wave.
>
> My kids won't stop complaining, and I have told them to knock it off.
>
> Worried about how something would look to others, I have lied.
>
> Missing a tag at the self-checkout line, I have pretended to scan it and put it in my bag.
>
> Frustrated with a coworker, I have talked about the person as soon as they left the room.

Not very Jesus-like living some days. But there is still hope!

In the church world, we go all out in our celebrations of the arrival of Jesus all those years ago, when He came in human form as a tiny baby. It's a bit weird to think of baby Jesus having His diaper changed, saying His first words, and moving from milk to solid food. Growing up just like a normal baby. Admittedly, not exactly how I often imagine the Savior of the world. But it's pretty incredible that He had this human experience because it means He literally knows everything it means to be human. Jesus faced frustrations, challenges, temptations, sorrows, and pain. Just like us. He handled it a bit differently, though.

> For we do not have a high priest who is unable to empathize with our weaknesses, but we have one who has been tempted in every way, just as we are—yet he did not sin. (Hebrews 4:15 NIV)

Jesus knew what it was like to be human, but He also knew what it was like to be in the kingdom, where there is no more pain, and all tears are wiped from our eyes in complete perfection. He understood that everything in this world is temporary. He lived differently because He knew that even though there will be sadness and joy in this world, nothing will compare to what awaits us in eternity. He also lived the mission to bring that kingdom into the midst of people He encountered. Jesus shared the miracles of the kingdom through healings and told judgy church people that the kingdom was already in their midst while they were busy following rules and trying to predict the future.

Where Jesus was present and doing the work of God, the presence of God's kingdom was evident. Do you want to know what's really incredible about that? Jesus has returned to the heavenly realm, but the presence of God's kingdom is still here! When we live like Jesus, on a mission for the kingdom and empowered by the Spirit, we continue to bring heaven to earth.

We still lie to people we love, flip our middle fingers, and gossip down the hallway because we lose sight of the incredible promise of the kingdom. We allow temptations and weaknesses to rise up and control our words and actions. But it doesn't have to be like that! We have the power within us to live like Jesus.

So let's hold each other accountable and be intentional about living and loving more like a child of God who has been created in the image of perfection and promised life eternal.

Lessons from the Garden

And He said, who told you that you were naked?
—GENESIS 3:11A MEV

WHERE ARE YOU HIDING?

I won't leave the house without at least a little makeup on my face because the thought of everyone seeing my naked wrinkles is terrifying. But if we're honest, we often try to cover up way more than our pores most days.

We don't often talk about the grief, depression, or anxiety that make it hard to get out of bed.

We cover up lying, stealing, jealousy, and pride.

We don't want anyone to know about our marriage issues, infertility, or financial problems.

We make sure nobody knows about any guilt and shame from a choice we made.

We pretend to be confident, so our deep insecurities don't show.

We all hide something.

And it started in the beginning.

Adam and Eve were living the perfect life in a beautiful garden. Then one day, with some smooth talking from a snake, they disobeyed God and changed themselves and the world with a single bite. So they grabbed some fig leaves and hid. But they didn't even just grab fig leaves. They took the time to design and sew a new wardrobe: "Then the eyes of both were opened, and they knew that they were naked. So they *sewed* [emphasis mine] fig leaves together and made coverings for themselves" (Genesis 3:7 MEV).

It seems ridiculous at first glance that they would put so much effort into a makeshift cover-up, but is it really that crazy?

Ever been caught in a lie and before you know it, there is a whole script with characters and props woven into the storyline you've created to create a new narrative?

Ever made a huge mistake and before you know it, you have crafted a closing argument in your mind that would rival even those of the best attorneys?

We're not much different than Adam and Eve when they broke out the sewing supplies and crafted some fig-leaf fashion. And just like it doesn't often work for us, it didn't really fix anything for them either. God knew exactly where they were and what had happened.

After the forbidden fruit incident, God called out for Adam and Eve, asking where they were. He knew exactly where they were, but He wanted them to respond. We are supposed to respond to God's Word too.

It can be hard to drop the fig leaves and step out into the open when we are so used to hiding our mistakes and imperfections. When we are used to trying to appear perfect. It can also be intimidating to respond because God will hold us accountable when we step out from our hiding places and stand face-to-face with Him, just like Adam and Eve were. But that's not a reason to hide. That is actually the reason we should respond to Him.

God doesn't hold us accountable for the sake of judgment and punishment. He does it with grace. He calls out in love, asking us where we are while we try to hide something shameful or painful.

When we respond, He heals and provides so that the fig leaves we grabbed and fashioned in a hurry are no longer necessary.

Trust Him enough not to cover up and hide. Be naked, and enjoy a stroll with your Creator who has known and loved you since the moment you were formed. No more fig leaves required.

Connection and Conversation

We give Eve a really hard time because it didn't take a lot to convince her to eat from that tree. But how often have we heard that sneaky voice talking us into things we know are against the direct commands of God in our lives? Now, if he showed up in the form of a creepy snake looking me in the eyes, I could avoid him. But do you know how Satan shows up to me? He shows up as that little voice in my mind. He affirms insecurities, makes up lies, and reminds me of things that I'd rather forget. He is so good at talking to me and even better at talking me into all sorts of things. So I end up hiding a lot.

I hide behind believable excuses, rehearsed explanations, jobs, kids, a fun personality, childhood stories, well-crafted personas, and so much more. Hoping that I'm not the only one who does this, let's look at the exchange with God in the garden with Adam and Eve from that perspective, knowing that we've been caught hiding plenty of times.

Read Genesis 3:8–11. Notice what two questions God asks when He is looking for them in the garden: "Where are you? Who told you that?"

God knew where they were, so take some time and consider why you think He would ask them these questions. Write down some times in your own life when you feel as though God has asked you these questions. What was your response?

God asked a lot of questions throughout the Bible. He didn't ask them because there was something He needed to know. God actually asked questions because He wanted the person being questioned to think a little deeper and figure something out about who God really is. Here are other examples to read and consider. Check out the question, and then read the whole conversation surrounding it, writing down what you notice about the circumstances and the responses.

> Exodus 4:2—"What's in your hand?" God asked Moses this question when he was afraid to confront Pharaoh and lead God's people out of Egypt. All he had in his hand was a walking stick, but it was one that he had used for many years as a shepherd and one that God would use to perform miracles. The question was to show Moses that he was already fully equipped to do what he was called to do.

> Jonah 4:9—"What do you have to be angry about?" God sent Jonah to save the people of Nineveh. He refused at first but eventually agreed to go after being thrown overboard, ending up in the belly of a whale, and then spit up onto the beach. But after the people of Nineveh listened to Jonah and changed their ways, Jonah basically threw a pity party. He wanted the wicked people of this city to suffer. So God asked him this question to highlight that he had been more than willing to accept God's mercy for himself but selfishly wanted it withheld from others that he decided were not worthy of the gift. God doesn't work like that, His grace and mercy are for everyone. He's not mad about it, so we shouldn't be either.

> 1 Kings 19:9—"Why are you here?" God asked Elijah that question as he hid in a cave, desperate to escape the wrath of an angry queen. Elijah was a

prophet of the Lord who had just publicly stood in front of a crowd and been witness to an incredible miracle that set God apart from all the pagan gods. It was an incredible event, and Elijah was victorious in the name of the Lord. But Queen Jezebel was mad that he had defeated and murdered the other prophets, so she put out a threat on his life. Elijah was scared, so he ran away. He ended up in the wilderness and, feeling overwhelmed and defeated, begged that his life be over.

God found him hiding in a cave and asked this question.

Elijah responded that everyone has messed up, and he did what was right but was left alone and in danger. God told him to get out of the cave and stand on the mountain. There was a strong wind, an earthquake, and a raging fire blowing past the mountain. And then, in just a whisper,

"Why are you here?"

The same question was asked again, but this time God told him to go back through the wilderness and finish His work. God still had plans for Elijah, even though he was hiding in a cave because of fear and frustration.

Elijah lost sight of God, just like Adam and Eve. Just like us.

Maybe the responsibilities of life are overwhelming, or the consequences of poor decisions threaten to harm you. It can feel comforting to isolate ourselves and simply hope that it's all over soon. But God doesn't want any of us hiding behind a bush or in a cave. He still has plans for us! Take some time to really consider what those plans might be for your life. What is God asking you right now?

DID YOU KNOW THAT GOD MADE CLOTHES TOO?

It's kind of wild to think that clothes weren't a trend until a piece of fruit changed the perspective of Adam and Eve. They suddenly felt shame in their fearfully and wonderfully made bodies and hid, requiring something to cover themselves.

While I can relate to the shock they must have felt seeing themselves as naked for the first time, their nakedness really should have been the least of their concerns since they hadn't listened to the Creator. The ripple effect of that would be felt throughout the rest of humanity in all sorts of painful ways. There would be pain and suffering, floods and fires, turmoil and wars, losses and lessons. Life now even came with an expiration date.

With their new knowledge, they could no longer remain in the sanctuary of the garden. They were kicked out of paradise to essentially start over in a broken world with some scary new knowledge. But in His abundant grace, God paused to make them a more durable set of clothes to replace the fig leaves they had pieced together: "The Lord God made garments of skin for Adam and his wife and clothed them" (Genesis 3:21 NIV).

When we don't listen to God, there are often consequences. There are ripple effects of pain and turmoil, shame and the desire to hide, loss and loneliness. There is also God in His abundant provision, ready to make us some new clothes for our new circumstances. He loves us so much that He provides for us even when what we need is a direct result of our mistakes and disobedience.

God crafted an expensive new wardrobe for Adam and Eve so they could walk out of the garden wearing clothes to cover what they were never meant to know. Their clothes were made from animal skins, which means their disobedience actually led to the first sacrifice, one made on their behalf to cover their shame. A life was lost so they could be clothed. That's a serious new wardrobe.

What happened in the garden was just the beginning. We continue to wear clothing based off the trend started all those years ago. But something has changed since that first taste of shame in the garden.

There has been a new beginning. Jesus was born into this world. He had been present at the time of creation and then arrived in human form to expand the story. Perfect in every way, Jesus carried all our imperfections to the cross and wore them for all to see, and now clothes us in a garment of grace. This grace doesn't mean you have nothing to hide; it means you have no reason to hide. The ultimate sacrifice was made on our behalf to cover it all. We can now be clothed in righteousness and grace, perfectly tailored and prepared to replace the tattered and worn-out garments of our sins.

Life is going to end for all of us, and animal skins won't last forever either. But when clothed in righteousness, we are prepared for eternity. If you're still wearing animal skins, this is the perfect time for you to change your clothes and discover the righteousness designed for you on the cross.

Continuous Creator

Therefore, we do not lose heart. Though
outwardly we are wasting away, yet inwardly
we are being renewed day by day.
—2 CORINTHIANS 4:16 NIV

WHAT DO YOU DO WITH
STALE BREAD?

I usually just throw it away, honestly. But recently, I was feeling creative when I looked at the stale hamburger buns buried in the back of my refrigerator. With a little luck and a lot of oil, I actually transformed them into some pretty incredible croutons. As I munched these crunchy bites on top of my salad, I was thankful that I hadn't given up on the hamburger buns that didn't seem like they had anything left to offer.

What if I told you that we can be like those stale, old hamburger buns?

Paul wrote a letter about transformation, saying that anyone who is with God gets a fresh start and is created anew. Our old lives are gone as new ones emerge. Paul knew about that personally. If you read the book of Acts, you're first introduced to Paul as the one hunting down people who believed in Jesus and making sure they never spoke His name again. Literally one of the worst enemies the early Christians had, gathering them up and standing to watch while they were murdered. But then Paul encountered God on a road one day. Paul was knocked off his horse by a bright light and heard the voice of God. The abbreviated version of Paul's conversion is that this blinding introduction to God transformed his life, and he went from a persecutor of Christians to a proclaimer of Christ.

We see through the life of Paul that God is a Creator who specializes in transformation, working from the inside out.

In the beginning, we were created and designed in the image of God. But because of sin, humans often appear less than holy. We make choices based on the desires of our hearts and bodies, rather than on our perfect Creator. Except for Jesus, who lived perfectly as man in a broken world. The disciples had the benefit of literally walking alongside Him and learning from His example. We now have their words and stories to guide us through those experiences and receive the same guidance.

When Jesus died, He rose from the grave and told His followers that He was returning to heaven. But He promised they would receive someone who would remain with them. The Spirit arrived with a grand entrance and remains in this world with each person who places his or her trust in Him and receives the gift of grace provided through the sacrifice of the cross.

The very first believers of Jesus, the same ones who were enemies of Paul before he was blinded by the Light, were the first ones to experience the visible presence of the Holy Spirit in the world. This experience of the early church was a final introduction to the transforming plan established by God and available to all of us, empowering us to be fully transformed.

So what does that have to do with croutons?

Just like those hamburger buns, we were created with a purpose, but we can only last so long on our own. These bodies have expiration dates, but the presence of God can transform us and make our lives new. We can go from stale buns to crunchy croutons with new life. We can go from broken bodies to eternal beings.

Created by God, saved by Jesus, and transformed in the Spirit.

Connection and Conversation

Paul wrote many letters. In fact, if you open a Bible to what we call the New Testament, you will most likely be reading something written by Paul. He is credited with writing the majority of the second half of the Bible, which is pretty incredible for someone who started his career persecuting people who followed Jesus. Let's take some time to read through his origin story and better understand how he got to a place where he could proclaim the transformational power of God.

And Saul was consenting to his death. (Acts 8:1 MEV)

This simple statement is our introduction to Paul. It might be a bit confusing because the verse refers to him as Saul. But that's because he actually starts as Saul and becomes Paul later. The name change is part of his transformation story, so we'll get to that. But let's rewind and read some specific passages because that statement from Acts 8:1 obviously refers to something pretty important. As you read, take notes specifically reflecting on the interactions between people. Recognize the various emotions experienced and the range of responses that people have to others and to God.

- Meet Stephen—Acts 6, 7
- A glimpse of Saul—Acts 8:1–3
- Meeting God—Acts 9:1–9
- Ananias reluctantly meets Saul—Acts 9:10–19
- Saul preaches—Acts 9:20–22
- Saul makes new friends—Acts 9:26–28
- Paul preaches—Acts 13:13–52

So that's literally just the beginning of Paul's incredible ministry. He went on to preach the gospel in modern-day countries like Israel,

Greece, and Italy. He also wrote lots of letters to the churches that he established, following up on concerns and encouraging them as they navigated what it meant to live in a world saved by Jesus Christ. But it started with him ravaging the church and dragging people off to prison, standing to supervise while they were executed for proclaiming the name of Jesus. This all changed when God showed up and literally stopped Paul in his tracks. God called him by name and transformed him from a persecutor to a preacher.

Go back to the readings, and take a few minutes to compare Acts 7:1–53 and Acts 13:13–52.

The first passage is a speech by Stephen as he stood before the religious people in charge. He was a man identified as being full of faith, wisdom, and the strength of the Holy Spirit. He was also being accused of speaking against the Law and everything held holy in those days. Serious accusations, but his response is powerful and unapologetic as he proclaims the history and hope of God's continuous plan for creation. Paul would have been one of the people in that crowd, infuriated by what they were hearing, and would have participated in throwing him out of the city and ending his life for what was being said. Then we read the second passage, a speech by Paul following a church service in the synagogue. It holds a lot of similarities to what was being said by Stephen not too long before this. There is a history lesson of God's people and a condemnation for those who turn away from the gift offered to us through the sacrifice of Christ and receiving the Spirit.

Paul was now preaching what he had previously prosecuted. Talk about an incredible transformation! To learn more about who Paul became on that road to Damascus, I encourage you to keep reading about Paul in the book of Acts, while also looking at some of the letters he wrote amid his missionary journeys and from the confines of a prison cell.

- Check out Acts 16, in which Paul and Silas were freed from prison in Philippi. Then read the follow-up letter he wrote to the Philippians while imprisoned in Rome.
- Take time to read another of his letters written from prison, this one to the Ephesians, after learning about their incredible experience with the Spirit in Acts 19.
- Read through Paul's letter to the Romans, and then read in Acts 27 about the shipwreck experienced on his way to Rome.

God chose Paul. He chooses you too. It doesn't matter what you did or how you did it. If he can take the man who literally executed Christians and transform him into a world-class preacher, He can take your mess and turn it into miracles.

DO YOU REMEMBER LOSING YOUR FIRST TOOTH?

Losing teeth can sometimes be sort of traumatic. It's usually a little painful when the tooth is removed from the original place it held in your mouth. And then there is a big gap left behind until the new one fills that space.

Joseph is someone who experienced big gaps for a while. He was seventeen years old and had ten older brothers who hated him because he was their dad's favorite. He also didn't really do himself any favors in how he interacted with them. They hated him even more once he told them about a dream he had in which he was in charge, and they were bowing at his feet. Maybe not the best choice when you have a brood of jealous older brothers. But he told them anyway. They threw him in a pit and then sold him off to Egypt.

For the next thirteen years, he was sold into slavery, hit on by a beautiful married woman, and sent to prison. Literally, everything seemed to be going wrong since interpreting that dream to his brothers all those years ago. At this point, his status and safety were removed, along with his integrity and influence.

Talk about some intense gaps.

But Joseph found himself standing before Pharaoh because the man in charge needed a dream interpreted and heard that Joseph was his guy for the job. The dream Joseph interpreted for him was about a famine, so he was put in charge of distributing food throughout the land.

One day, familiar faces showed up. They belonged to his brothers, who bowed at his feet, just like his dream had shown all those years ago. After some back and forth, Joseph revealed who he was, and healing took place. Their relationship wasn't just restored to what it had been. It was renewed in beautiful ways.

I'm guessing we've all experienced painful gaps and empty moments. People leave and places change. Sometimes the removal is painful, and we wait in the gap for a promise to be filled. But it doesn't always come as quickly as we'd like. Joseph experienced slavery, lies, and prison before the gap was filled.

This may be hard to hear, but sometimes the painful gap is necessary. Just like it takes a new tooth time to grow, we need time for growth too.

Could God work instantly? Sure! But we learn a lot during the gaps. Joseph learned humility, self-control, patience, and honesty in his gaps. The same boy who bragged about his dream to a group of jealous brothers was gone. In his place stood a man who could now offer forgiveness and grace to those same brothers.

Removal and renewal can take longer than we'd like. But if you are in a gap now, know that God is using it for your growth and your good. His process of removal and renewal is one of healing from a loving Creator, who continues to expand all that He has promised.

A HEALER WHO REACHES THE DEEPEST WOUNDS

"Do you want to be healed?"

That probably feels a bit like a trick question if you have ever been sick, damaged, or broken in some way. But this is exactly what Jesus asked a man who was lying in a crowd of sick people. They were all waiting on the side of a pool that promised healing bubbles—but only to the first person who entered the swirling waters each time.

The specific man in question had been sick for thirty-eight years and hadn't yet made it into the water. Stop and think about that. Thirty-eight years. Sick, just lying next to a pool surrounded by other sick people.

So how did he respond to the question from Jesus? Well, he simply said that he couldn't get in the water on his own and had nobody to help. Not exactly an answer to the question, but it sounds like a logical excuse. He wanted to be healed but couldn't figure out a way to do it other than lying by this pool and hoping help would come along. Luckily for him, help came along, and the bubbling pool was no longer even necessary.

Jesus told him to stand up, and he was healed. Just like that. No bubbles needed.

The pool boasted healing waters, but Jesus offers a different kind of water. He offers living water that is available for all who desire it, not just the first one to reach Him. Jesus explained it like this to a woman at a well in need of deliverance: "The water that I give will become in those who drink it a spring of water that bubbles up into eternal life" (John 4:14 NIV).

Living water will heal all wounds and quench all thirst because it holds the promise of eternal life. Most healing goes beyond physical wounds and diseases. The healing we really need is for brokenness woven deep into our hearts and minds. Pain and suffering from sin. Living water is the cure.

But you have to want it. You have to want the Healer. That's what Jesus meant when He asked, "Do you want to be healed?"

Living water can't be found in a bubbling pool or pouring from a faucet. It is found by knowing the One who sacrificed everything for our healing.

> He personally carried our sins in his body on the cross so that we can be dead to sin and live for what is right. By his wounds you are healed. (1 Peter 2:24 NLT)

If you need healing today, don't just wait by the pool. Unwrap your wounds, and join me as we meet Jesus. Stand up and be healed.

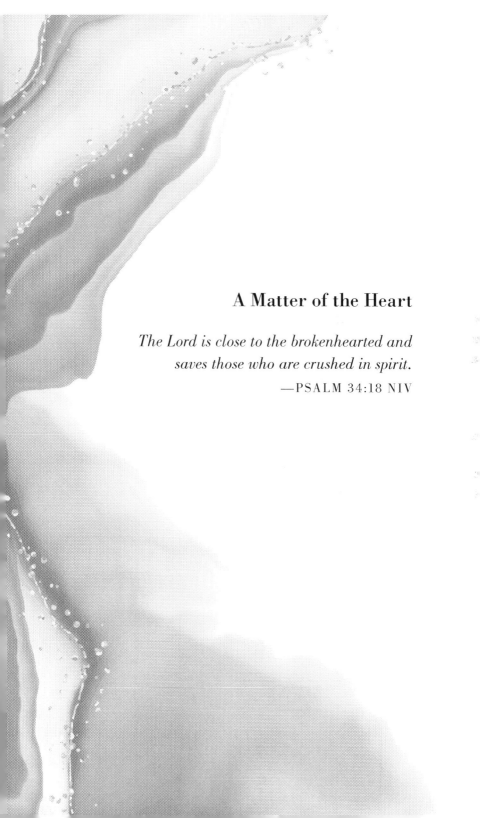

A Matter of the Heart

The Lord is close to the brokenhearted and saves those who are crushed in spirit.

—PSALM 34:18 NIV

HAS YOUR HEART EVER FELT HEAVY?

"It is with a heavy heart …"

That phrase never ends well because it is usually the introduction to bad news.

But we don't always announce our heavy hearts, do we? In fact, most of us do everything we can to carry the heaviness around without letting the strain show. We shoulder the weight of grief, shame, loneliness, guilt, loss, anxiety, sorrow, and stress. Often covering the grimace with a smile and hoping that nobody will notice.

There is the book of Wisdom in the Bible (more commonly known as the book of Solomon) that tells us laughter and smiles can conceal a heavy heart, but when the laughter ends, which it always does at some point, the grief remains. It's not enough to conceal a heavy heart so others don't know. It's still there, and it's still heavy.

So how do we lighten the load?

Think of it like stepping into a swimming pool. No matter what the scale says, when you are surrounded by water, you end up feeling weightless.

Jesus taught that if we believe in Him, we will have rivers of living water flowing from our hearts. This living water is God's presence. Though circumstances may not change, just like the number on the scale doesn't actually change in a swimming pool, our hearts experience being weightless when flowing with living water.

All our heaviness can be lifted in His presence. But it's not always that easy, is it?

It's usually a little uncomfortable for most of us to put on a swimsuit and step into a pool. There is this required amount of exposure before getting in and experiencing the relief of being immersed and weightless. It's the same with the presence of God through living water. We must be willing to share what we've been trying to conceal and expose ourselves fully to the Spirit. But once immersed, we are able to experience an inner feeling of having the weight lifted.

And the most amazing part about living water is that you never have to get out of the pool! The feeling of being weightless can last with God. That's an incredible promise when you've been struggling under the weight of a heavy heart.

Connection and Conversation

If you grew up going to church, you have probably been taught many parables. They were the stories Jesus told that were about something familiar with the intention of teaching a new concept or making something clear about Him and the kingdom of God. If you aren't familiar with parables, they're a great place to start when opening the Bible because they are pretty easy to read, and most of them come with some explanation. So you also learn the lesson Jesus was trying to teach the people originally hearing them too.

We're going to spend time with one parable right now, but here are a few others I recommend reading and writing down the lessons being taught. Sometimes the parables are found in multiple books of the Bible, what we call the Gospels, so I'll include all the places to find them. You can take your pick when you start looking them up.

- Good Samaritan—Luke 10:25–37
- Lost sheep—Luke 15:4–7; Matthew 18:10–14
- Prodigal son—Luke 15:11–32
- Workers in the vineyard—Matthew 20:1–16

Take your time with them. Look through the Gospels (Matthew, Mark, Luke, John), and see what other parables you can find. They are great tools for learning and sharing a lot about Jesus!

But now, let's dig a little deeper into a parable commonly referred to as "the sower." Pull out a Bible, and read through this story from one, or all, of the following passages. As you're reading, pay attention to the four types of soil. They are going to be important details in understanding what Jesus was teaching. The passages are Matthew 13:1–23, Mark 4:1–20, and Luke 8:4–15.

Jesus said that a farmer planted different sets of seeds. Some were trampled and some were snatched by the birds. Others couldn't grow because rocks blocked their roots. A few of them were choked by weeds. The others found the good soil and grew into an impressive crop.

But Jesus was talking about more than seeds and soil. He was just using them as a metaphor to talk about God's Word and our hearts. The condition of our hearts.

Sometimes His Word doesn't even make it into hearts before the enemy steals it. Other times, we pile so many activities and plans into our lives that we don't leave room for the Word to really grow. We often allow the worries of life and the pleasures we desire to choke the Word so that it can't survive. Life can be complicated. The rocks and thorns can be overwhelming, but the good soil is a heart that's prepared for God's Word. A place where it can grow.

> Keep vigilant watch over your heart, that's where
> life starts. (Proverbs 4:23 NIV)

We need God's Word because it tells us and shows us how to live. It's not just a ton of rules that we need to follow so that God will love us. It actually helps us to live the abundant lives He wants for us. When His Word takes root in our hearts, it even changes the lives of people around us by what it's able to produce. But our hearts need healing to be a healthy place for God's Word to thrive and grow.

Luckily for us, God is an incredible gardener. He tends to our hearts with living water that offers nourishment and renewal. His light shines to reveal new truths and understanding. He patiently cultivates and cares for our hearts until we are prepared to receive His Word. Is your heart ready?

WHAT IS YOUR HEART
SPEAKING TODAY?

Everything that comes out of the mouth starts with what is in the heart. Jesus told us that. He was in the midst of ministry, feeding over five thousand people with a few loaves of bread and a couple tiny fish. And He was doing it while walking on water and healing all sorts of people. Miracles were evident wherever Jesus went as He preached and taught throughout the land. But then He encountered some religious people who thought they knew everything.

They literally started an argument with Jesus because they caught His disciples not washing their hands before they ate. Yeah, they were worried about some guys not washing their hands after Jesus literally walked across a body of water. But it wasn't that they were worried about germs. They were worried about the Law and general rules of religion not being followed.

Jesus responded, noting how they are hypocrites and violate laws that contradict their own laws. He also quoted the prophet Isaiah by saying, "These people honor me with their lips but their hearts are far from me. They worship me in vain; their teachings are merely human rules" (Matthew 15:8–9; Isaiah 29:13 NIV).

Jesus wanted them to know that you can say all the words, do all the things, go to church every Sunday, post all the Bible verses on Instagram, and wear the church merch, but it's not actually about any of that!

It's not about the rules. It's about your heart. But why does your heart matter so much?

What is in our hearts doesn't just stay there. It eventually comes out of our mouths.

Jesus explains that it's not what goes into their mouths that makes them unclean, it's what comes out of their mouths. Back then, they followed many laws about what and how they could eat, identifying certain animals and combinations of food as considered unclean. Jesus is telling them that they need to be worried about what is coming out of their mouths instead of focusing so much on the laws that say what can go into their mouths.

Simple enough, right? Except that James, a follower of Jesus, points out that our tongues often let loose with a wild combination of blessings and curses: "And so blessing and cursing come pouring out of the same mouth. Surely, my brothers and sisters, this is not right!" (James 3:10 NLT).

We hold a lot in our hearts that eventually ends up on the tips of our tongues. Sometimes we make snarky remarks or shout less-than-holy words before we even realize they had been bubbling beneath the surface.

Luckily, God made our hearts and understands everything they do. He also desires that we get closer to Him so that our hearts can be fully renewed through relationship with Him instead of hoping that we can simply follow enough rules to be considered good.

Think about what your heart has been speaking lately. If it's more curses than blessings, give God a chance to love you a little deeper today, and see if your heart starts to sound a little different.

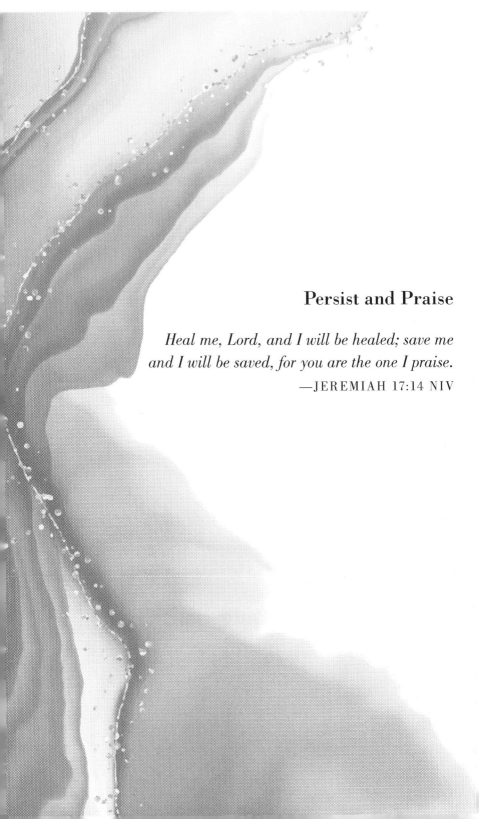

Persist and Praise

Heal me, Lord, and I will be healed; save me and I will be saved, for you are the one I praise.

—JEREMIAH 17:14 NIV

WHAT DO YOU DO WHEN YOU'RE SICK?

I went through this stretch where I was really sick for what felt like a long time. Not to be dramatic, but it was a miserable couple weeks. From the cough to the body aches, I had been frustrated by it all. But as those symptoms healed, I was left with a strained pain in my neck that limited my ability to move and interact the way I liked. No medicine or treatment seemed to relieve it, so I usually ended up just whining on the couch with a heating pad.

But before I was fully healed, my daughter's birthday rolled around, and she wanted to go sled riding. So I mustered all my strength and paused my whining for an afternoon. Then, as I stood at the top of that snowy hill, I thought about Paul.

In one of his letters to the church of Corinth, he referenced a thorn in his flesh that had made him physically weak. Never specifying exactly what it was, people have made assumptions that it was a physical issue or just a general reference to the hardships he faced. Either way, he referred to this thorn as something he begged for God to remove more than once. But then he began to recognize that there was a gift in this weakness because it allowed him to be in touch with his limitations.

This has always been difficult for me to understand because I'm someone who likes to rely on my skills and talents, rarely attempting to do anything that isn't a guaranteed success based on what I know that I can do well. But lately, amid this sickness and other circumstances, I've been learning a lot of lessons about my weaknesses. My neck pain being the least of them.

When Paul talked about his weaknesses and suffering, he could have spent hours complaining about the pain he was enduring and the issues he was having. Think back to what you read about his life, and you'll recall that he would have had a lot of examples to offer. Multiple beatings, prison sentences, and a shipwreck would give him enough material for a long list of complaints. But instead of doing that, he usually talked about rejoicing. He talked about real joy, not just that pretend happiness we use to cover up our pain.

As much as our problems make us aware of our weaknesses in the moment, they can also help us understand a more eternal hope if we take the time to notice the grace surrounding us in the struggle. God shows up in amazing ways when we must rely on Him. That eternal hope can initiate a joy for the moment that overpowers our pain.

The thorn doesn't always go away, and the suffering doesn't always cease. I know that's not the healing answer we all hope for, but the promise of a restorative God brings hope that can feel like flying down a snowy hill in pure joy, allowing us to at least forget about the pain for a moment.

Connection and Conversation

Take a moment to think about the past twelve years. Consider significant moments, persistent issues, celebrations, losses. Try to guess how many lives you have encountered in that time and the way you intertwined with people you don't even know exist. Crazy to think about, right?

Well, we're told by a few gospel writers about a two people whose lives intertwined, and they didn't even realize it. But they both encountered Jesus in ways that would change them forever.

Take some time to read about a bleeding woman and a ruler's daughter. You can find them discussed from a few different perspectives in Matthew 9:18–26, Mark 5:21–43, and Luke 8:40–56. As you're reading, take notes about all the people who encountered Jesus. Notice their demeanors and responses when interacting with Him. Also, make sure you are paying attention to how they respond when things don't go as planned.

A ruler in the synagogue had called out to Jesus when his young daughter was sick, believing that she could be healed. A woman who had been bleeding for twelve years reached out and touched His garment in a crowd, believing she would be healed.

Both believed, but the little girl died as the woman was healed.

This woman trembled in fear as Jesus called her out of the crowd to tell her that she had been healed and to go in peace. She had been bleeding for twelve years and violated all sorts of laws by being out in public in that condition. She definitely wasn't allowed to be touching anyone. When called out of the crowd, the woman would have been scared of the possible punishments related to the many laws she was violating by reaching out to Jesus in a crowd of people.

She was scared that the past twelve years of pain and suffering were only the beginning. She was scared that this was it for her.

She reached out to Jesus in faith anyway.

The family of the little girl told Jesus not to bother coming to their home anymore because all hope had been lost with her last breath. Jesus went to their house anyway. He told them she was simply sleeping as they scornfully laughed.

The child's family members were scared it was too late. They were scared the life they had envisioned was ending abruptly. They were scared that all hope had been lost. They gave up and laughed at Jesus in disbelief.

But Jesus spoke, and the little girl opened her eyes, alive and well.

Both stories intertwined with Jesus, had happy endings, and came with healings. But they were different. The woman led with faith despite her fear. The family, however, allowed its fear to cloud belief and lost hope before the healing.

Life can get really scary sometimes. Circumstances can change, hope seems lost, fear settles in about what was and what could be. When you are scared and overwhelmed, be brave. Reach out with trust that He has healing in His hem.

Don't be afraid, just believe. (Mark 5:36 NIV)

HAVE YOU EVER MET ANYONE MORE PERSISTENT THAN A CHILD IN NEED OF SOMETHING?

I haven't. My kids will say some variation of "Mommy" over and over and over until my complete attention is on them. Kids can teach us a lot. Jesus Himself said we must approach and receive God like little children. Part of that is in our persistence.

Jesus told a story about a widow who was persistent in her pursuit of support from a judge. He didn't give her the time of day, but she returned with her request over and over and over again. The judge finally responded.

> I care nothing about what God thinks, even less what people think. But because this widow won't quit badgering me, I'd better do something and see that she gets justice. (Luke 18:4–5 MSG)

I have often had the same reaction as that judge, if I'm being honest. Rolling my eyes with a deep sigh while I answer the persistent requests of my kids. Responding in a way that is selfish, impatient, and unkind.

That's not God's response with us.

Soon after telling this story, when Jesus was out and about, He passed a blind beggar. This man began calling out to Him. As the crowds tried to shush him, the man remained persistent. He called out until Jesus responded.

"What do you want me to do?" Jesus asked.

The man wanted to see.

"Your faith has saved and healed you!" Jesus responded.

Immediately, the man's sight was restored. No eye rolls or heavy sighs from Jesus. He wants us to call out to Him. He also wants to respond.

The response won't always be instant healing; we were never guaranteed that. But we are promised a Healer who loves us so deeply that He will hear our prayers, draw us close, and transform our lives in miraculous ways.

God is listening. Be persistent.

Scar Stories

*Give thanks to the Lord and proclaim
his greatness. Let the whole world
know what he has done.*

—PSALM 105:1 NLT

DO YOU HAVE A FAVORITE PICTURE?

I can get lost in an old photo album for hours, thinking about the shared memories with the smiling faces. It's one of my favorite feelings to sort through the highlight reel of life with the people I love most in this world. But photo albums don't show everything. Our pasts often include words we wish had never crossed our lips, choices we desire to rewind and do differently, encounters in the dark that we hope never come to light, hurt that never quite went away, and moments that end up more bitter than sweet. What do we do with all of that?

Paul wrote a letter to the Philippians while he was chained up in Rome. He packed a lot into this letter, but part of it was a quick guide on how to get over it and move on.

Step 1: Forget what is behind.

Step 2: Reach forward.

Forgetting is honestly very hard for me. I often replay scenarios in my mind, going over and over what could have been different. That usually just leaves me frustrated and exhausted. But God has advised that we don't need to remember the old stuff anymore because He's doing a new thing. He's all about renewal, transforming past pain into future blessings.

Jesus talked a lot about the new things God was doing. To prepare everyone for all these new things, he once reminded them that you never put new wine into old wineskins. Why? Because the old wineskins had already been stretched and worn out, so new ones were needed if the wine was going to be held: "And no one puts new wine into old wineskins. For the old skins would burst from the pressure, spilling the wine and ruining the skins. New wine is stored in new wineskins so that both are preserved" (Matthew 9:17 NLT).

But in typical Jesus style, He wasn't really talking about wine.

If there are moments that have stretched and worn you out, it's time for something new. God is trying to bless you in ways you can't even imagine, but you need a new way to hold on to them. Give up the old wineskins. Let them go. Forgive yourself and others. Release the bitterness and regret. Let go of the past decisions, mistakes, and missed opportunities. Lean into God and heal.

He wants us to forget about the pain and problems of the past so that we can reach forward for Him. While you're reaching forward, you'll be amazed how you won't even be able to look back. You'll be too busy gazing on God's promise for the future.

Forget what is behind, and reach for something new. The future is fresh and ready to be filled with His blessings.

Connection and Conversation

"This little light of mine …"

Did you ever sing that song? Vowing to always let your light shine, adamantly refusing to cover it. I don't know about you, but I honestly never really understood what we were singing about. Let's dig around in the gospel of John and figure it out so we know exactly what light we are shining and sharing.

Check out John 8:12. Then look up these verses, too, writing down something you notice that is similar throughout all of them.

- John 6:35
- John 10:9
- John 10:11
- John 11:25–26
- John 14:6
- John 15:5

What did you notice about all of them? They all contain an "I Am" statement. Jesus is identifying Himself to everyone He encounters, letting them know who He is. Letting them know who God is.

Go back a little further in the Bible to the Old Testament. Read Exodus 3.

God was leading His chosen people out of slavery and told Moses that if he encountered any issues to simply state that he was sent by, "I Am who I Am." Fast-forward to Jesus, and He is giving more clarity to that I Am through these statements. Jesus is walking and talking and showing us exactly who God is.

But these I Am statements don't stop there. They extend to us. In John 8:12, when Jesus tells His disciples that He is the Light, He also says that we can have the light when we follow Him. So we hold His light with us and within us. This light is meant to shine into the world so that everyone around us can experience the true light through us. A light that can overpower all the darkness this world has to offer.

I think we can all agree that there's a lot of darkness, which means we need a lot of light. As a kid, I'm not sure what I thought would stop this light from shining as I was singing. Now that I'm an adult, I know there are many things that can cover the light.

Discouragement, embarrassment, and disappointment. Just to name a few.

But have you ever felt like it wasn't that your light was covered, more like it was broken?

I once received a candle as a gift, and literally moments after pulling it out of the packaging, I watched as it smashed on the floor. My first thought was that it was ruined and unusable. Broken and shattered.

But after the glass shards were safely in the garbage, I went home with my broken candle and burned it as though it were still fully intact. It was still my favorite scent from my favorite store, so I wasn't willing to give up on it. The light wasn't ruined by the broken jar holding it.

Have you ever described yourself as broken? Maybe you've experienced a breakup, illness, or job loss that left you feeling damaged. Broken and shattered.

Well, just like my candle, the light isn't ruined by our brokenness. God is not deterred by a little damage. God looks at you as His favorite, even if there are a few cracks. He will pick you up and continue to use you as a light in the darkness even when you feel too broken to be of value anymore.

It's His light. Let it shine.

DO YOU HAVE ANY COOL SCARS?

Most of my scars have been collected from surgeries and C-sections, but I do have a big one on my knee reminding me of the time I saved a little kid from an epic mud puddle. Admittedly not a really cool story, but the scar definitely serves as a reminder of it anyway. If you've ever had a scar, you know that most of them come with a story. Jacob was a guy who knew something about that. His wasn't so much a scar, though, but more of a limp.

Here's a bit of his story.

Jacob had been on the lookout for a blessing ever since he held his brother's heel coming out of the womb. He fooled this brother into trading his birthright for a bowl of soup and then tricked their dad into blessing him instead of his brother. He was so desperate for a blessing that he risked a curse.

Quite a few years after the soup incident, Jacob found himself in a wrestling match with God, desperate for a blessing again. But this time he isn't trying to sneak a blessing. Instead, he is hanging on for dear life.

"I will not let go unless you bless me." That was Jacob calling out during a wrestling match with God. His hip gets messed up in the fight, but he receives the blessing he so desperately needed after a life of struggling and manipulating. Jacob was given a fresh start in life, but now it came with a limp.

Like a wrestling match with God, some scar stories are almost too wild to believe. Jesus had a story like that.

Put your finger here in the wounds of my hands. Here—put your hand into my wounded side and see for yourself. (John 20:27 TPT)

That's Jesus, showing His wounds from the cross to His disciples. Jesus shows up to show off his scars because the story was too wild to believe. Jesus wants the disciples to see those wounds to understand the pain He experienced. He wants them to realize that He walks away with wounds in His hands and side but that it was all worth it because a blessing is offered to us. That is also a little too wild to believe.

While scars come with a story, they also usually come as a result of pain and require healing. Jacob figured this out as he was wrapped up in a late-night wrestling match. Jesus showed the disciples that when He held out His hands, His pain comes with the promise of our healing.

A new start with a blessing doesn't always look perfect or feel great. Sometimes we are left with a limp or wound to remind us of the story. Some of our scars aren't visible, or the stories may seem unbelievable. But they are there to serve as evidence of the promise.

Show the scars and share the story.

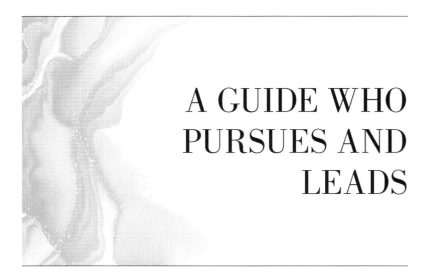

A GUIDE WHO PURSUES AND LEADS

True confession: I'm a terrible driver.

I've been driving a new car, and it has a feature that sends out an alarm anytime I drift on to the line meant to guide me. It even gently nudges me back on the road! But since getting this car, that alarm has become an all too familiar sound, a constant reminder that I am drifting. It's an annoying feature to have on a car, but I have to admit that it's also pretty helpful.

The truth is that I've always been a terrible driver. I was in high school and on my way home from a friend's house one dark and rainy night. I was going around a curve and selecting a new CD when I suddenly found myself driving up an embankment and landing in the middle of a cornfield. I called my parents to rescue me. The rain was still coming down as my dad had me walk through the cornfield to collect all the detached pieces of metal. It was a traumatizing night, to say the least. I can't help but think that if my car had one of those annoying alarms to warn me that I was coming close to the side of the road, I could possibly have avoided a lot of frustration and damage.

But maybe the real issue is that I didn't totally change my ways after that cornfield incident because my current car tells me that I still drift. A lot.

I drift a lot in my car. And I drift a lot in life, if I'm being honest.

In the second book of Hebrews, there's a reminder given that we should be attentive to what we have learned so that we don't drift away: "We must pay the most careful attention, therefore, to what we have heard, so that we do not drift away" (Hebrews 2:1 NIV).

We can drift from what we've been taught and told in all sorts of ways, ending up far from the path God intended us to be on. We can drift into a job, relationship, addiction, or all sorts of other places and look back, wondering how we ever got there. But the author of Hebrews has a suggestion about drifting so that we don't end up in a cornfield, picking up the pieces of wreckage.

The author goes on to say that our sins come with consequences, but there is also the opportunity for great salvation. This promise comes along with some amazing gifts. The Spirit of God moves into our hearts. We are guided with signals and nudges that keep us on the intended path.

On our own, we drift like a distracted teenager behind the wheel. But the Spirit wants us to correct some things before we end up in the cornfield. And it gives us the gifts and guidance to make that possible.

Join me as I share some insecurities, and we meet some inadequate people from the Bible, including a guide along the way who pursues us in our brokenness and leads us toward His promises.

Competently Called

He has saved us and called us to a holy life, not because of anything we have done but because of his own purpose and grace. This grace was given us in Christ Jesus before the beginning of time.
—2 TIMOTHY 1:9 NIV

WHY HAVE YOU SENT ME?

Moses asked God this question when he was sent to Egypt on a mission to save God's people from slavery. Feeling unequipped and inadequate, Moses wasn't sure how or why any of this was even happening. I imagine Moses's pleading prayer whispered through clenched teeth as he sees the people of Israel covered in mud and worn from the sun, not sure what to do next.

Can you relate? Ever found yourself in a situation that doesn't make any sort of sense? Felt like you stumbled into the wrong place even though you thought for sure God told you to be there?

I can! There was this one time when I started a new job that was typically filled by someone who had different education and expertise than I did. Throughout a rigorous month of training, I felt really inadequate as I prepared for an exam required to fill that role. My struggles and issues didn't disappear, but during that time, I found comfort in reading the story of Moses and knowing that I was not the first person who ever felt that way.

I hope you can relate too. If you feel unequipped and inadequate, you are in the perfect place because God has a habit of using inadequate people.

> A murderer who couldn't talk very well led His people out of slavery.

> A fisherman with a temper preached to over three thousand people.

> A childless woman who was a hundred years old gave birth to a nation.

Imperfect is an understatement. But these people prove in all sorts of ways that it is in our weakness that we learn how to trust God. Moses led an entire people out of slavery and introduced them to God in some very powerful ways. Peter would establish the church, bringing over three thousand people into relationship with Christ after his very first sermon. Sarah would birth the baby who would establish generations of God's people.

Lives were changed by these imperfect people when they were willing to follow the call and allow God to use them. When God called them, they were just people. People who get old. People who lack what is needed to get the job done. People who doubt. People who stray. People who make all sorts of mistakes. But God had plans for them anyway. He blessed them, babies were born, and people were saved.

God will make us promises, and we will always be inadequate to carry them out on our own. But is anything too difficult for God? Nope! So if you are feeling inadequate, join the club! Remember His promises, and prepare to be amazed with what He can do with imperfect people willing to trust Him.

Connection and Conversation

I'm not a beach person, mainly because I hate the sand. But I can't sit on a beach, with sand sticking to all my nooks and crannies, without thinking of God's promises. He made important promises to an unlikely couple that involved counting grains of sand and counting on Him to follow through with what He said.

Let's take some time to read a little deeper into the promises of God woven into Abraham's life and the impact those promises continue to have in our lives. As you are going through these passages, write down what God is promising and what He is asking for in return.

Start with Genesis 12:1–9

This is the first encounter Abram has with God. Notice his name: Abram. He'll eventually become Abraham, but that's part of his calling, which comes later. Also notice that God promised a lot and didn't ask for much, just that he go to the land shown by God. Highlight the verses where God makes His promise. Now, as you read Abram's response, keep in mind that he was seventy-five years old, with no kids at this point. But he listened and he went. Abram, his wife, Sarai, and his nephew Lot followed the call.

Next, Genesis 12:10–13, 18

Over the next few years, Abram would go through family issues with his nephew, panic during a famine, offer his wife to Pharaoh, and just really kind of do his own thing in the midst of following his call from God. Highlight the verses where God shows up and reiterates His promise to Abram. God appeared to Abram at various times, but there came a point when they needed to have a serious conversation about what has been promised and what is to come.

On to Genesis 15:1–6

Do you hear Abram's doubt? He's telling God that he doesn't understand how any of these promises can be true because he still doesn't have any kids, and his servant is going to end up being his heir. Sound familiar? I know that I've mumbled similar things under my breath about circumstances and situations I thought were going to work out sooner, yet it seemed like nothing was happening. But notice God's response. Go back and look at the promises you have already highlighted. Sound familiar?

Now, Genesis 15:7–21

They participate in a blood covenant ritual. It sounds pretty gruesome to us but it was an understood practice to Abram. This type of covenant would have been done to seal a promise. Two people would walk together between the animals and through the blood, symbolizing their seriousness in the covenant and representing their fate should they violate what they promised. Abram was instructed to take a variety of animals, cut them in half, and lay them opposite each other. After doing this, though, Abram fell asleep, and we're told that a great darkness and terror came over him. But while he was in this darkness, the Lord showed up and reiterated His promise for blessings, heirs, and land. Then a smoking pot and flaming torch, symbolizing the presence of God, passed through the blood to seal the covenant.

God demonstrates in that moment that He is going to lead the covenant. He is offering grace and simply asking Abram to have enough trust to go where he is sent, even if it is unclear.

Read Genesis 16; 17; 18:1–15; 21:1–7

Abraham received a promise from God. He was told that lots of babies and plots of land were in his future. But he was childless and getting older by the day. As mentioned earlier, he was seventy-five years old when God first told him to look at the stars and count them as a promise of the descendants to come. But he was ninety when the impatience got the best of him. He took matters into his own hands, with the encouragement of his wife, and had a baby with his servant.

So now, with Ishmael born in his name, it was time for God's promise to be fulfilled, right? Nope.

God promised to care for Ishmael and his mother as they were scorned and shamed. But they weren't part of the covenant promise He made with Abraham while gazing at the night sky. That promise was for Abraham and his wife, Sarah, to multiply in God's intended timing. It took another ten years—when Abraham was now one hundred years old—for their son Isaac to be born.

To anyone watching, Ishmael and Isaac were both sons of Abraham. It honestly wasn't even unusual to have multiple baby mamas back then. But these babies were different in a very important way. Ishmael was born from man's impatience; Isaac was born through God's faithfulness.

Ishmael was cared for and blessed but was never part of the covenant promise with God and Abraham. That was reserved for Isaac. That was the promise God made. Abraham thought he could move things along because God just didn't seem to be working fast enough on providing those descendants He promised. But that's not how it works.

While it's easy to judge Abraham for his deceit and doubt, we do it all the time too. We jump into things and make choices, assuming God will jump in with us and make it all work out. But it doesn't really work like that. Even if we go rogue and make choices based on our preferences rather than His promises, God loves us enough to still offer good things and blessings, like He did with Ishmael. But when we follow His guidance and have enough patience to trust His faithfulness, we will experience the full glory of His plans. And that's when we realize it's better than anything we could have imagined or accomplished on our own.

It took twenty-five years for Abraham and Sarah to understand all that God promised. Twenty-five years of Abraham struggling to keep it all together. Twenty-five years of grace are evident in the covenant God established with Abraham. Twenty-five years of God saying, "I've got you." Twenty-five years of God simply asking for enough faith to follow Him.

So what does that mean for us?

The covenant established with Abraham and his willingness to go laid the framework for continuous blessings and a legacy that led to all the ends of the earth. The same ends of the earth where the followers of Jesus were told to go and make disciples. The same ends of the earth where the early church was built. The same ends of the earth we are still called to reach.

And now, as we are called and promised and sent, we have the benefit of a new covenant.

Find Hebrews 9:13–15.

Just like Abram in the darkness while God passed through the blood and established a covenant, we were in the darkness of sin while Jesus Christ offered His own blood and established a new covenant of eternal life, requiring no more blood to be spilled. He simply asked that we trust Him enough to go where He sends us. Consider where God is calling you to go. It might be down the street or across the world. Wherever it may be, He is simply asking that you have enough trust in His promises and faith to go where He leads and to follow His timing.

HAVE YOU EVER GONE FISHIN'?

My kids learned to fish a bit over the summer, and it got me thinking about the fishermen who answered a call way beyond their pay grade. If you read through the Gospels, four books written about Jesus in this world, you'll see many references to fishing. It was an important trade in many of the areas to which He ventured. The guys who fished back then would have been kind of rough and rugged. They mostly fished at night, staying out and hoping to bring back full nets in the morning. They made a good living but had to know what they were doing. They worked hard to put food on their tables and take care of their families. Their lives revolved around fishing.

Jesus called some of these fishermen as His first followers, telling them to leave their boats behind because He was going to make them fishers of men. But why would they walk away from their livelihoods to follow a guy around the countryside? All they knew was fishing. Which is exactly why Jesus referenced fishing in the calling placed on their lives: "Jesus said to them, 'Come, follow Me, and I will make you fishers of men'" (Mark 1:17 MEV).

Jesus was telling them that everything they put into fishing, He wanted them to bring into living life with Him.

All their grit and determination, bring it.

All their real and raw energy, bring it.

All their expertise and knowledge, bring it.

All their desire to care for others, bring it.

Jesus didn't want followers who had simply been created and curated in a crispy-clean church. He wanted real people to bring their real lives to follow Him. Fishermen could probably be identified by their appearances and behaviors, whether or not a boat was in sight. Jesus also wanted that in His followers.

He still wants that.

Jesus wants people who smell, look, and sound like someone who loves Him, whether or not a church is nearby. Be you; follow Jesus so others can meet Him. That's what it means to be a fisher of men. The fishing disciples were called to lead lives that showed others Jesus in their own unique ways.

That's our calling too.

Jesus is calling us from the classroom, the cubicle, the workshop, or the living room we find ourselves in. He is calling you to take who you are and what you do into the world in a way that helps others meet Jesus wherever you might be.

The Struggle Is Real

*Make me to know Your ways, O Lord; teach
me Your paths. Lead me in Your truth
and teach me, for You are the God of my
salvation; on You I wait all the day.*
—PSALM 25:4–5 MEV

ARE YOU SCARED OF THE DARK?

We often proclaim the empty tomb as an exciting place that reveals the most incredible blessing. But if you read about those discovering the empty tomb, it wasn't really a celebration for them. Each gospel offers a bit of a different picture, but all of them mention the fear and confusion experienced by Jesus's friends who stepped foot in that tomb.

"Where Is He?" "Who Rolled Away the Stone?" "Who Took Him?"

Their questions reveal a lot of doubt and not much celebrating.

If you rewind a bit, Jesus predicted His death and resurrection. He told His followers what was going to happen. But when it actually happened, it wasn't what they expected. He wasn't there. All they saw was a dark, sad, quiet, empty tomb. So they fumbled in their fear, sorrow, and confusion.

Then Jesus showed up!

We're told of Him talking in the garden, walking along a road, serving fish on a beach, and finding friends in the upper room. In some of these exchanges, they don't even recognize Him. They are so caught up in the darkness of the tomb that they completely miss Jesus in their midst.

They felt like God was missing in action when they needed Him the most. Sound familiar? It probably felt like standing alone in the middle of a miscarriage, divorce, bankruptcy, depression, or terminal illness.

Those are dark and empty tombs. It would be easy for anyone to get lost in them and feel completely alone in the grief and uncertainty. But when Mary and the guys were standing around feeling alone, Jesus was actually right there with them. He wasn't in the tomb anymore, but He spoke to them, fed them, showed them His scars, and reminded them of what the empty tomb truly held. Promises, it held future and fulfilled promises.

The tomb is important. It's where Jesus was laid following the sacrifice of the cross. The tomb was necessary, but it was also temporary. They were never meant to gather and weep at the tomb. Jesus had plans for them to go and proclaim what had been done and what that meant for each and every one of us.

Sometimes it's hard to understand the blessings when we are caught up staring into the tomb of our struggles, just like Jesus's friends. If you are stuck weeping at a tomb, know that God is waiting for you to turn around and see His face. He is there to walk with you and talk with you from the tomb to the blessing.

Connection and Conversation

Maybe you have lost your job, or the one you do have is overwhelming. Maybe your marriage is in shambles, or you just lost a spouse. Maybe your child is wrapped up in addiction, or you just experienced another miscarriage. Maybe your finances are a wreck or your anxiety is maxed out or you just said goodbye to your best friend.

Struggle comes in all shapes and sizes. We often feel like a failure amid the mess. But we trust in a creative God, who heals, provides, and redeems the mess. So our struggles are nowhere close to being a failure. Let's read a little deeper into the lives of some messy people God transformed for His glory so that we can learn how to see it in our own lives too.

Matthew 26:31–35, 69–75 and John 21:1–19
Peter denied Jesus and fled into the darkness of the woods, He met him on a beach for breakfast.

Acts 7:54–8:3; 9:1–19
Saul lost his sight on a dirt road after killing Christians. He was redeemed as Paul, and his vision was restored.

John 4:1–42
The woman at the well avoided everyone to try and avoid the shame. But she was offered living water that transformed her life as she ran into town, so everyone could see and know what she had discovered.

Genesis 18:1–15; 21:1–7
Sarah was barren for ninety years, until God told her she was having a baby. She literally laughed at

the news. But then Isaac was born, along with an entire nation.

John 5:1–18
A man sat crippled by a pool for thirty-eight years, hoping for healing. Then Jesus came, and the man walked into a new life.

2 Samuel 11; Acts 13:16–37
David impregnated a woman who was not his wife and killed her husband. But he became identified as a man after God's own heart, and his lineage led to the birth of Christ.

The struggle was real for them, and it is real for many of us. Struggle can feel as though we have messed up too much or missed our last opportunities. But God is so good that He pulls us out of the mud and guides us from the deserts we find ourselves in.

Struggle isn't a failure; it's an opportunity for God to show up in some pretty amazing ways. So if you are struggling, pick your head up, and see where God is leading you today.

WHO DO YOU TRUST
WITH YOUR HAIR?

When I was a kid, my grandma would do her own perms at home to save the cost of going to the salon. My sister and I thought it would be great if we could have curly hair, too, so Grandma agreed to perm our heads one summer at her house. Luckily, my sister is older and won the first spot in the bathtub with the permanent treatment. I watched in horror as my grandma chopped off all her long hair and gave my sister a perm matching her own. Imagine a seven-year-old version of *Golden Girls*. That was my sister. She loved it, but I was mortified. Since then, I have always been cautious with my hair.

I recently started dyeing mine for the first time ever, and it was really scary. Sitting at the salon with orange slime soaking on my head, I realized something and understood why I have held on to my straight brown hair for so long.

I was not in control, and that terrifies me.

Sure, I went in with a description of how I hoped things would turn out. But the reality is that it was not really up to me what happened for the next couple hours. The moment I sat down in her chair, my life was in the hands of the woman holding the scissors. I could make plans, but how I walked out of there was totally up to someone else.

As a self-identifying control freak, that is my worst nightmare! But as someone who also self-identifies as a Jesus lover, I've recently been learning how not to be in control all the time.

> You can make many plans, but the Lord's purpose
> will prevail. (Proverbs 19:21 NLT)

There have been times when I read that verse, and it sounded like a threat. Like no matter what I plan and want and do, God's plans are going to happen anyway. Whether I like it or not.

But it's not a threat at all. Rather, it's a promise. A very good promise.

As humans, it's our natural tendency to follow our own desires, thoughts, and cravings. I think if we're being honest, we can also admit that we don't always make the best choices.

I've joked that dyeing my hair was in response to a midlife crisis, which might be true because it all started after finding my first gray hair. But if I had tried to cover my gray hairs myself, it would not have gone well. I needed someone who knew what he or she was doing.

Finding a good hairdresser, one you can trust, is a scary process. You can read reviews, look at pictures, and get recommendations from friends. But at some point, you just have to sit down in the chair and trust the hairdresser.

Sometimes crisis—midlife or another kind—is the only way we'll be willing to let go of control and try to trust. Is there something you're trying to change today? Looking for help with an area of life that seems to be broken or out of control? Let me refer you to Someone who is incredible.

His promise for you is that He has a plan. No matter what choices you've made or where your plans have taken you, His purpose for you has not changed. Just trust Him. Sit down with God, and be prepared for the transformation.

Covenants and Clouds

*Whenever the rainbow appears in the clouds,
I will see it and remember the everlasting
covenant between God and all living
creatures of every kind on the earth.*

—GENESIS 9:16 NIV

DO YOU KNOW HOW TO SWIM?

God tells Noah to build a boat. People think he's crazy, but he builds it and brings on a collection of every animal and creature. The rain pours for forty days. A dove shows them the coast is clear, and a rainbow appears in the sky to remind them of God's promise that He'll never do it again.

It's a great story. But did you know they were on that boat for over a year? That is a long time to be floating around with a bunch of animals wondering, *What comes next?* I would be pacing the floor and peering out the window of that ark with anxious annoyance. I know that's how I'd act because I do that now when facing problems that don't seem to be moving out of the way quickly enough.

We still live in a broken world and still experience floods. These could be financial issues, relationship problems, health concerns, mental health struggles, and anything else that has wrecked your world. And just like making it from the flood to the rainbow, sometimes it can take a while for us to make it from the problem to the promise.

During the time of Noah, this world had been in turmoil since the downward spiral that started in the garden with a piece of fruit. God was grieving what He had hoped would be enjoyed by His children, who were instead filled with a desire for evil. God wanted something different for His creation and sought redemption through the floodwaters. It took time for the water to recede and required patient waiting to see what would be different when the land was revealed again.

It ended with a beautiful promise, but it wasn't really a happy ending because the flood didn't fix humanity. It didn't take long for them to start making bad decisions once their feet hit dry land. But since God promised to never wipe out humanity again, He tried something new.

He sent Jesus.

Rather than trying to remove sin and fix the world, He brought an eternal promise to all of us. Through Christ, our problems aren't completely removed, but they can be fully redeemed now in the process.

When problems arise, and it feels like you are trapped on a stinky boat waiting for the mud to appear, find a way to be patient and have hope. God's promises for us are better than ever. But He wants to make sure we are ready receive them, so there may be times when it takes a little while to clear the debris and prepare us for the dry land.

Connection and Conversation

I went on a trip to Paraguay when I was young and feeling like I was ready to tackle the world. I ended up in a makeshift medical clinic equipped with a basic ability to speak Spanish and a medical dictionary. Reality settled in as the first person sat down and started speaking something that wasn't Spanish. It turned out that many of the people still used their native language. So there we were, trying to find a connection somewhere between English and Guarani.

I've been thinking about this language experience and considering how it relates to what the church celebrates as Pentecost. Let's read together through the experiences of those first leaders of the church and their encounters with God in a brand-new way. As you are reading, try to imagine what it would be like to be the first people experiencing God like this. Consider how you would respond if you were part of the different groups represented in these precious moments when God's Spirit arrived.

Read Acts 1:1–11

Jesus died on the cross, left behind an empty tomb, and stayed with His friends for a while before returning to heaven. Before leaving, He promised that someone else would come to be with them.

Read Acts 2:1–12

As the disciples waited, Jerusalem started to fill with everyone assembling for one of the Jewish festivals that called for people from across the nations to gather at the Temple. This particular festival recognized the first fruits of the harvest and recalled the giving of the Law to God's chosen people.

Suddenly, the One promised by Jesus showed up with a loud rushing wind and flames for each of the believers. This commotion caught the attention of everyone else, so they came to check it out. What they discovered was a group of Jesus followers speaking their language. Literally. Suddenly, every language from the nations that had gathered could be heard.

Read Acts 2:14–41

With no language barriers, Peter was able to preach a powerful message that led to the baptism of thousands. People who came to remember the Law were now given the Spirit. They weren't held to a book of rules and laws anymore. They were offered a guide to dwell within them. So are we!

Pentecost shows us what a powerful and incredible gift it is to follow Jesus and receive the Spirit. It also reminds us how necessary it is for us to find a way to share that message.

When I was in that clinic, we didn't always understand each other. But when the message was clear, there were tears and hugs filled with understanding and hope. That's what it can be like to share about a risen Savior who loves and lives with us. It is confusing and hard but totally worth it when the connection is made.

ARE YOU A PEOPLE WATCHER?

I used to hate going to the gym. I hated the way my thighs rubbed together and my arms jiggled. I would look around the gym and see examples of people who had succeeded while I was failing. Not super motivating. But something changed as I started looking around differently. Although my thighs still rub together, now I kind of actually look forward to being in the gym.

In the book of Hebrews, the author talks about a great cloud of witnesses. There is a list of names and experiences that showcase God's care and guidance over the years. They include Abel, Noah, Jacob, Joseph, Moses, Rahab, David, and many more.

It's an interesting group of people all gathered on the same list. Some were murdered while others were murderers. Some were prostitutes and others adulterers. Some immediately obeyed God's Word, and others needed more convincing. But they were all identified as people who were faithful.

Not perfect. Faithful.

So what does this have to do with the gym?

I looked around the gym yesterday and noticed something. We were all there to work out our bodies, but we were all different. Some were trying to lose weight, while others wanted to bulk. Some were looking for a place to socialize, while others wanted to be alone. Some just wanted a place to listen to true crime podcasts without interruption and burn off some anxious energy.

Thinking back to the cloud of witnesses, we are encouraged to run a race surrounded by them. I've come a long way, but if you told me that everyone in the gym was going to head out into the parking lot and run a race together, I would hide in the bathroom until it was over. Luckily with the great cloud of witnesses, it's not a foot race. It's also not a race against anyone else. We each have had a race designed just for us. The cloud of witnesses are not there as opponents. They are there to provide examples of faithfulness, evidence of God's love, and encouragement for the difficult stretches.

So who is in your cloud? God created the course that He designed you to run. He also provided people who have finished their races and can now run alongside you. Take some time to figure out your course and gather your cloud. Go where He leads with confidence in your ability to do all that He has called you to be.

A PROVIDER WHO WITHHOLDS NOTHING THAT IS NEEDED

Are you so worried about what you want or what you think you're missing out on that you lose sight of everything else?

I do. All the time. I worry, compare, stress, and panic a lot.

Life and social media have ways of showing you exactly what you want and, therefore, making you feel like you'll never get it all at the same time. It's a dangerous combo. Life can feel desolate and hopeless pretty quickly when we are consumed with thoughts of everyone else's best and fixated on our worst.

But we are loved by a God who created us and continues to provide exactly what we need. The proof is all around us.

> If God gives such attention to the appearance of wildflowers—most of which are never even seen—don't you think he'll attend to you, take pride in you, do his best for you? What I'm trying to do here is to get you to relax, to not be so preoccupied with getting, so you can respond to God's giving.

People who don't know God and the way he works fuss over these things, but you know both God and how he works. Steep your life in God-reality, God-initiative, God-provisions. Don't worry about missing out. You'll find all your everyday human concerns will be met. (Matthew 6:30–33 MSG)

The wildflowers and the birds show it to us in the way God cares and provides for them so they can grow and thrive with barely any effort on their parts. If He does it for the flowers and wildlife, we can be guaranteed that He does it for us too!

If you're feeling at a loss or less than today, go for a walk and find some flowers. Take a deep breath, and remind yourself that God has already provided and will continue to offer all that you need. That is a guarantee found in the simple scents and sounds of nature. All you have to do is look around for the evidence.

Join me as we walk through the fields of life and consider all that God has provided us.

Living in the Dark

*The light shines in the darkness, and
the darkness has not overcome it.*
—JOHN 1:5 NIV

HAVE YOU EVER FELT
THE DARKNESS?

Growing up in the middle of nowhere, there were many mornings spent waiting for the school bus in the pitch-black, surrounded by nothing at the end of the driveway. It was so dark that you could feel it. It was almost like you could reach out and hold it in your hand.

> Stretch out your hand toward the heavens, so that there may be darkness over the land of Egypt, a darkness which can be felt. (Exodus 10:21 NIV)

That is God speaking to Moses as he repeatedly attempts to free the people from Egypt with increasingly terrible plagues. God knows the power of darkness, and as Moses lifted his hand, a thick darkness spread across the land so that the people couldn't even see what was directly in front of them.

In the beginning, the earth was formless and completely dark. The first thing God knew it needed was light. He saw that the light was good. Darkness remained, but light was provided to the world. God has always known the power of light and will use it to His glory and for the good of His people.

Going back to the plagues and Moses, God provided light in the dwellings of His people living in Egypt as the world around them went into a deep darkness. While the people of Egypt were forced to remain lying for days in the darkness, the children of God were able to freely move about their homes. They were held in His light during that time, shielded from the depth of darkness that existed around them.

But I think we can all admit that it's hard to keep the lights on when the world us around can be rally dark sometimes.

Disease. War. Loneliness. Violence. Depression. Poverty. Political Feuds. Injustice.

> I am the world's Light. No one who follows me stumbles around in the darkness. I provide plenty of light to live in. (John 8:12 MSG)

That's Jesus.

God didn't stop with light at the time of creation; it wasn't just about the sun and the stars. He sent Jesus to be the Light and share the light. For the whole world. All the time.

The world doesn't stop being dark. But we are promised light to live in, just like the Israelites had when the plague of darkness was all around them. The darkness, no matter how heavy it may feel, can't overtake us when we are surrounded by the Light. When we follow Him and live in love and obedience to His example, we find freedom.

Connection and Conversation

We went to see an immersive art exhibit once. It was one where you walked into a large open space and watched as the colors swirled and changed around you, perfectly timed to the music that was playing. The artwork was visible around, above, and below us. We were perfectly immersed in the beauty and experience. But about five minutes into the show, the room went dark. All the beautiful colors that had been swirling around us suddenly disappeared.

You could hear groans and mumbling around the room as everyone waited to see what would happen next, frustrated that it was not going as planned. It made me think of the Israelites as they emerged from the parted Red Sea and found themselves in an empty desert. I can only imagine what it was like to walk through the walls of water with swirling colors and intricate scenes, immersed in a perfect example of God's provision as they escaped slavery in Egypt, only to find themselves coming out on the other side in a desert with no water to drink or food to eat.

If you're familiar with the Israelites' journey, you know that God provided for them every time a need arose in the desert. You probably also know that they spent a lot of time complaining about their time in the desert. Lots of groans and mumbling. If you're not familiar with their grumbles, check out the following passages from the book of Exodus. Write down what they were lacking, how God provided, and their responses. We can learn a lot about our own grumbling when we take time to reflect on their journey with God in the desert.

The Route of Escape—Exodus 13:17–14:31

We see God's provision and care from the moment they escape Egypt. It tells us in this passage that God knew they would become fearful if they approached battle right away and may have been tempted to turn back. This was a group of people who had been working tirelessly their entire lives with minimal food and provisions. We can assume they were worn and weary at the beginning of this journey. God was protecting them by leading them into the wilderness.

When have you been able to look back on a situation and realize that God was guiding you somewhere you wouldn't have gone on your own, but you can now recognize it was for your good that He took you in that direction?

As they approached the waters of the Red Sea, I'm assuming their hearts filled with fear and their minds with dread. It would have looked like an impossible situation. Then the armies of Egypt came racing toward them as Pharaoh had changed his mind again and demanding their return. They began to panic and proclaim that they wished to be back in Egypt, certain their fate would be somehow better in the pits of slavery than standing on the beach. But the Lord directed Moses, and He lifted His rod to separate the waters so they could walk through on dry land. If you read the story of creation in Genesis, it tells us that God separated the waters and the land. Here he is doing it again on behalf of His children. He is a creative God, who will continue to divide and conquer on our behalf.

Think of a time that seemed impossible, with no way out. How did God provide a way? What did God divide and conquer on your behalf in those circumstances?

Waters of Marah and Elim—Exodus 15:22–27

So they are three days into this journey and with no water. My mouth gets dry just thinking about it. There was a day recently when we went to an amusement park, and I didn't pack enough water. That afternoon felt like an eternity, so I'd definitely be grumbling after three days in the hot sun with no water. To make it worse, the first water they come across is bitter and not drinkable. What does God do? He sweetens it so they can drink. Then He leads them to a beautiful place with wells and palm trees. It's starting to feel like a vacation!

When have you gone without something and become bitter at the thought of it? Will you let God touch that place in your heart today and sweeten it for you?

Hunger Takes Over—Exodus 16

They are about a month and a half into the desert journey, and they are hangry. The people start complaining again. Their complaints haven't changed much since they stood on the beach, staring at the Red Sea. They dream about going back to Egypt, where there was food and life was easy. Wait, what? They were slaves! The life expectancy of a slave in Egypt didn't go much beyond thirty. That was not an easy life. But now that they are surrounded by sand and traveling on empty stomachs, they lose sight of the promise and provision.

What are you dreaming about from your past that isn't actually as good as you want to remember it? Look around at your current circumstances, even if they aren't perfect. Write down at least five ways God has provided for you since stepping out of that past your mind keeps wandering back toward.

God loves His children and wants to provide for them. So He told Moses that they would have meat in the evening and bread in the morning. They were blessed with quail each evening and flakes of bread each morning. The quail was familiar and easy to understand. But they had to ask, "What is it?" when the bread showed up. They called it manna and were told to gather only what was needed for that day. Some gathered more, trying to store and save what had been given. They found out pretty quickly that it would spoil and rot the day after it arrived. God wanted them to learn that He would provide, and He would continue providing exactly what they needed. They were to trust Him enough to go to bed with empty bowls, relying on His provision for the next day.

Have you ever felt the need to gather and store the good things in your life in case it all comes crashing down the next day? Many of us do this with money and possessions. What would look different in your life if you didn't cling so tightly to your dollars and trusted that God would provide what was needed daily?

Still Thirsty—Exodus 17:1–7

Here we go again. They are complaining about being thirsty and reverting to their cries of wondering if they were just brought out into the desert to die. It's getting hostile when God instructs Moses to strike a rock, and water begins to flow. It sounds dramatic and chaotic, a group of desperate people seeing only a dry desert laid out before them.

Have you ever let the panic set in and asked, "Are you even here with me, God?"

A lot of people groaned, mumbled, and left when the lights went out in the art show. But has it ever felt like that in life? Everything was going great, and then suddenly, the lights go out.

> Maybe you were enjoying the thrill of a new pregnancy only to find out there was a miscarriage.

> Maybe your relationship that felt like it was meant to last forever has left you sitting alone.

Maybe your dream job closed its doors and left you with a severance package.

Maybe it just seems like everything that was meant to be is disappearing quickly.

Life can get dark sometimes.

When life went dark for the Israelites, they forgot about God in the midst of their desert. They struggled to remember His provision that took them along the dry land between the walls of water. Many who walked that path did not make it to the place that was promised to them because they couldn't get back on track because of their grumbling and doubt. They started to make choices and place their hopes in places other than the promises of God. A journey that was meant to take a few months ended up taking forty years.

I don't know about you, but I don't want to get lost in the empty darkness. I want to make it into the places God has promised. So what should we do when the lights go out?

- Stay immersed, even when it's dark.
- Don't give up and grumble.
- Remind yourself of all that has already been provided for you.
- Trust that God is still providing and that the lights will come back on.

HAVE YOU EVER HIT ROCK BOTTOM?

We use that phrase when talking about being at our absolute worst. It can look like Elijah hiding in a cave hoping for death or Peter fleeing into the woods after denying Jesus. It can resemble the woman thrown into the dirt after being caught in adultery or the man waiting for healing at the side of a bubbling pool. It can feel like Hagar rejected in the desert with her baby boy or Mary and Martha weeping at their brother's tomb.

Sorrow, fear, pain, and frustration usually accompany the experience of hitting rock bottom. But Jesus told a story about two builders and a rock bottom that sounds a little different. One of them built his house on sand, and the other one chose a foundation of rock. They encountered a storm, and the beach house was quickly destroyed, while the one with a rock bottom could not be shaken.

Jesus was actually giving them advice to build themselves on a solid foundation of His Word. He knew that would give the solid structure needed to protect them through the storms and struggles of life. This idea of God as the Rock would have been familiar to those listening. David wrote a lot of psalms referencing Him in this way.

> The Lord is my rock, my fortress, and my savior;
> my God is my rock, in whom I find protection. He
> is my shield, the power that saves me, and my place
> of safety. (Psalm 18:2 NIV)

David knew a lot about rock bottoms. He impregnated a woman who wasn't his wife and murdered her husband. He was chased by his best friend's dad, who also happened to be the king. He battled many enemies and endured waves of sorrow. But He also always turned His attention back to the God he knew could conquer and provide.

Jesus knew this, too, and recommended a rock foundation because this specific Rock is not simply a slab under a building. He's a solid base that offers protection and power. So when the storms rage, we can be built on and surrounded by the One who has promised to withstand the storms with us.

Do the work now to dig deep and build a solid foundation with God so that when you hit rock bottom—because we all do at some point—you'll have exactly what you need to stand solid through the storm.

Won't He Do It?

*And we know that in all things God works
for the good of those who love him, who
have been called according to his purpose.*

—ROMANS 8:28 NIV

HAVE YOU EVER FELT LIKE SOMETHING WAS MISSING FROM YOUR LIFE?

What if I told you that it could all change if you were willing to go searching for some donkeys?

Sounds crazy, I know. I'm not really telling you to go looking for donkeys, but there were some missing a long time ago, and they belonged to a rich man who had a really handsome son named Saul. He was sent out to search for the donkeys but couldn't find them anywhere. His partner in the search party suggested that they go check out a seer, someone who could give them a message from God.

This particular seer was Samuel. He had been told by God to find a king for the Israelite people. While Saul was out looking for donkeys, Samuel was out looking for a king.

When their paths crossed, it became apparent that Samuel was looking for Saul. So while he was simply searching for lost donkeys, he ended up becoming anointed as king. That's quite an upgrade. But if Saul hadn't sought direction from God in finding the donkeys, he never would have met Samuel, and he never would have become the king of God's people.

So what are your donkeys?

> Lost identity during motherhood.
> Uncertainty about which career path to follow.
> Wishing for a partner in life.
> Finding a purpose in retirement.

While you are out looking for the job, the right person, or the source of fulfillment, are you seeking God too?

God will help you find the donkeys. But He might also have some bigger plans in mind. When Saul left to find the donkeys, he never planned to return home as king. What you thought was missing could be something that you never could have even imagined. Keep looking for the donkeys, but be intentional about seeking God, and you will be amazed at what He can provide.

Connection and Conversation

A lot happened in Samuel's life before he found a king looking for some donkeys. In fact, a lot happened in Samuel's life before he was ever even born, things that set him on the path where he encountered Saul. There are a couple books of the Bible believed to have been written by Samuel. They are named after him and provide us with much information about the establishment of the monarchy in Israel. They also show us a guide to faithfulness in a crazy world. But it all starts with his mom, Hannah. Take note of how she is described.

Read 1 Samuel 1:1–20

Hannah is identified as a woman of sorrow. We're told she is bitter, and tears are pouring from her eyes. But what does she do repeatedly?

She talks to God!

Hannah takes her pain and pleads to God through prayer. She is blessed with a baby boy. He is named Samuel and taken to be placed in the care of Eli, the priest.

Read 1 Samuel 1:21–28

Hannah dedicates the baby to the Lord. Read again what she says in verse 26: "I am the woman who stood here praying."

She is identified by her prayer, by her conversation with God. Now her child is identified by that prayer as well.

Read 1 Samuel 3

Samuel is now a young boy and identified as ministering to the Lord. He is confused at first when hearing the voice speaking to him in the night because he is not yet familiar with the voice of God. But he is called by name. He is called by God. What started with Hannah's prayers is coming now to Samuel in the night as he responds to the voice of God, saying, "Here I am." He then shares the Word of God with all of Israel.

Read 1 Samuel 7:2–17

If you want to read about some of the chaos that occurred with the people of Israel, go back and read chapters 4 through 6 as they describe the ark of God being captured by the enemies of Israel. The ark held the sacred presence of God and is eventually returned in a crazy way after men were killed and some came away plagued by tumors. It's an incredible testimony to the power of God and the honor due His presence.

But back to Samuel.

He's older now, and called upon as Israel realizes they have messed up and need some help getting right with God. Notice his instructions to them: "If you are returning to the Lord with all your heart, then put away the foreign gods from your midst. And make firm your hearts unto the Lord, and serve Him only" (1 Samuel 7:3 MEV).

Consider these simple instructions. Put away everything that is not of God. Place your heart with God. Serve Him with everything you have. Those are good instructions for us too. How can you apply them to the distractions, frustrations, and temptations in your own life?

Read 1 Samuel 8

Samuel is an old man now, and his sons haven't exactly followed in his footsteps. The people of Israel are getting worried about what will happen when he's gone, so they tell him that he has to find a king. So what does Samuel do?

He talks to God!

After some back and forth, God tells him to "obey their voice, and make for them a king." There is back and forth because God wants them to rely on Him. But they are demanding a person in whom to place their trust. Not exactly the relationship God wanted to establish with His people. Remember, just a few verses ago, when Samuel encouraged them to place their hearts with God and serve Him alone. Seems like they've already strayed from that. But He allows them the choice to move in that direction.

Read 1 Samuel 9

We made it to the donkeys!

Read 1 Samuel 10–11

Saul is anointed in the name of the Lord and finds his donkeys. That's really a win-win situation for him. And as if it couldn't get any better, we're told that when he turns from Samuel, he is given a new heart. Saul was changed that day. He was transformed into a king anointed by God.

Spoiler alert: Saul doesn't exactly follow through on everything that God, Samuel, and the people of Israel hoped he would. You can find out all about it if you just read a few more chapters in 1 Samuel.

Read 1 Samuel 12

Samuel is getting old and saying his final goodbyes to the people of Israel. He gives them words of wisdom, like a loving grandparent who only wants what is best for his children. As a servant of the Lord, he truly wants what is best for His children. Samuel encourages them to obey the voice of God. His mother called out to God on his behalf, and God, in turn, called on him. From the moment he heard God call out to him as a young boy, Samuel was faithful in his calling. It wasn't easy, and it wasn't always what people wanted to hear, but Samuel listened and repeated what he was told by God. He also never stopped praying for the people of Israel, no matter how much they messed up.

Let us all walk away from 1 Samuel with this command of the Lord that He spoke through His servant, Samuel: "Fear the Lord, serve Him in truth with all your heart, and consider what great things He has done for you" (1 Samuel 12:24 MEV).

HOW BRAVE ARE YOU?

It's not always easy to follow God. Sometimes it involves following Him out into the field looking for donkeys and coming back a king. But it sometimes involves stepping into a fiery furnace, one so hot that it ignites the guards pushing you into the flames. Trusting Him can involve stepping into some pretty intimidating places without confirmation that it's going to work out in the end. That's the truth. You see, there was this group of guys who showed us a lot about what it means to bravely trust God as they were thrown into a fiery furnace because they loved God and refused to bow to a statue created by the king to honor him instead.

It's a crazy story that we talk about a lot in the church world because they survive being thrown into the fire. But what's even crazier than them surviving is the statement they made before getting tossed to the flames.

> If we are thrown into the blazing furnace, the God we serve is able to deliver us from it, and he will deliver us from Your Majesty's hand. But *even if* [emphasis mine] he doesn't, we want you to know, Your Majesty, that we will not serve your gods or worship the image of gold you have set up. (Daniel 3:17–18 NIV–)

They firmly believed in God's power to save them from the flames. They also loved God enough to trust Him even if He didn't do it.

Whoa.

Believing God can do something is one thing. Trusting Him with the option to not do it and loving Him regardless is next-level faith.

Most of us don't have the risk of being tossed into a furnace, but there are other fires that can surround us.

The flames can show up as someone dying, divorce, losing your job, miscarriage, serious illness, anxiety, and so much more. When you are facing some of these flames, could you make an "even if" statement?

> I will love You even if my marriage crumbles.

> I will serve You even if I lose my job.

> I will trust You even if my bank account is empty.

> I will follow You even if the diagnosis is bleak.

Those statements are hard to make. They require trust that goes beyond comfort and hope that reaches past what's good in the moment. But God set the example and did one better: "God clearly shows and proves His own love for us, by the fact that *even though* [emphasis mine] we were still sinners, Christ died for us" (Romans 5:8 NIV).

We didn't earn what took place on the cross. Instead of waiting until we were enough, God proved how much He loves us by doing it anyway. The ultimate sacrifice has already been offered for all of us even though we didn't deserve it. He's an "even though" kind of God, while we're still figuring out the "even if."

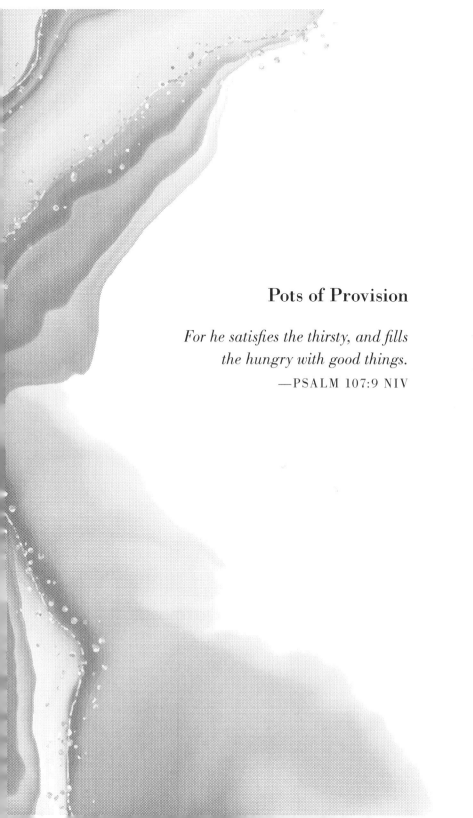

Pots of Provision

*For he satisfies the thirsty, and fills
the hungry with good things.*
—PSALM 107:9 NIV

HAVE YOU EVER DONE SOMETHING CRAZY WHEN YOU WERE HUNGRY?

We have a tendency to be angry, irritable, whiny, and overly dramatic when we miss a meal. But making crazy choices when you're hungry isn't new.

> Look, I'm dying of starvation! What good is my birthright to me now?" (Genesis 25:32 NIV)

That was Esau trading his birthright to his brother for a bowl of soup.

A birthright was a big deal. It was about more than just getting a great inheritance. The birthright put you in charge of the family and territory while promising a special blessing from God. But Esau gave all of that away for a mediocre bowl of lentils. He literally sacrificed his future for some soup.

Seems crazy, right? But we do this too.

We often desire something that feels better in the moment and give away something that God has planned for our future. Sometimes it's intentional. But sometimes it happens without much thought through our quick decisions and impulsive actions.

But God wants more for us.

> Don't waste your energy striving for perishable food like that. Work for the food that sticks with you, food that nourishes your lasting life, food the Son of Man provides. He and what he does are guaranteed by God the Father to last. (John 6:27–28 MSG)

The food provided in Jesus Christ is our life-sustaining salvation. It goes beyond our earthly needs and grumbling stomachs. It gives us life for all eternity.

He wants us to stop seeking temporary relief by sacrificing permanent blessings. Put down the bowl of lentils, and patiently wait for His provision.

Connection and Conversation

As people, we generally give in to our cravings. There are all sorts of temptations swirling around us that tap into our desires and insecurities, offering the cure for whatever ails us in that moment.

Hungry? Stop at a fast-food place on the way home, even if dinner is already in the Crock-Pot.

Lonely? Call that person you know will always pick up, even if it's not for the best reasons.

Insecure? Gossip with your coworkers so they can notice someone else's flaws and not your own.

Anxious? Drink an extra glass of whatever soothes your nerves.

From the moment Adam and Eve bit into the fruit that changed the world, our abilities to resist temptation have only become more challenging. Temptations are all around us, on our screens, and in our phones. Even though Jesus didn't have to deal with social media and everything that comes along with our digital world, He faced temptations head-on in a very real way and gave us a great example of how to not just avoid temptations but how to stand against them.

Grab a Bible, either a paper one or digital, and find Matthew 4 or Luke 4. Both gospel writers walk us through Jesus being tempted in the wilderness. I'm going to be using Matthew 4 for references. Do a quick reading of the entire section. In Matthew, that is Matthew 4:1–11. Write down or highlight anything that catches your attention. Now, go back and read just the first verse:

> Jesus, full of the Holy Spirit, left the Jordan and was led by the Spirit into the wilderness. (Matthew 4:1 NIV)

There is a lot packed into that one verse. It's important to understand what happened right before this, so go back a little bit and read Matthew 3:13–17. There you will learn Jesus was baptized in the Jordan River by his cousin, John. During the baptism, the clouds part as the voice of God is heard, and a dove arrives to represent the Spirit. It's a powerful moment when God is present in His entirety as Jesus is presented and now fully prepared for ministry.

But immediately following this incredible expression of God, the Spirit leads Jesus into the wilderness. Did you catch that? The Spirit led Jesus into the wilderness. It wasn't an accident that He ended up in the desert. He didn't just get lost. He was led there. By the Spirit.

Can you think of anyone else God led into the wilderness?

The Israelites. You're right!

Go all the way back to almost the beginning in your Bible and read Exodus 14:21–31 and Exodus 15:22.

Do you notice the similarities with Jesus in Matthew 4? They pass through the water and are led into the desert, facing temptations and frustrations.

We've talked about the Israelites a few times already and how they ended up stuck in the desert, wishing they were back in Egypt as slaves. God provided, but they continued to complain. They even turned their jewelry into idols they could worship, looking for anything that would save them from the struggles of the desert. They failed in the wilderness. There's really no other way to put it.

They didn't trust God, and they failed, ending up in the desert for forty years.

But now Jesus is in the desert. Matthew tells us that He was there for forty days. Not quite forty years, but still long enough to feel a little desperate in the hot wilderness without food or water. Let's see how He responds to temptations and frustrations.

Temptation 1

The devil is identified as the tempter, and he is taking an easy shot at Jesus's hunger, suggesting that He turn a stone into bread and satisfy His hunger. How does Jesus respond? With the Word of God.

Look up Deuteronomy 8:3. Now read Matthew 4:4.

Physical food is not sustenance, at least not for the long term. Jesus is saying that God is what sustains. He is able to look past the temporary and see the eternal. He can deny His physical hunger in pursuit of something that will truly satisfy. Could He have turned those rocks into loaves of bread? Probably. But His miraculous works weren't intended for His benefit. They were only for the purpose of inviting others to participate in God's glory, and simply fulfilling His hunger on that hot day in the desert wasn't going to accomplish that. So He remained hungry for the sake of true satisfaction.

Temptation 2

The devil takes him to the Holy City. Standing on the highest point of the temple, the devil tells Jesus to throw Himself off and have the angels catch Him. Now this is where it gets a little tricky. Look up Psalm 91:11–12, and then read Matthew 4:6. The devil is actually using scripture, God's own Word, to convince Jesus to give into temptation and have His life saved in a spectacular way. But how does Jesus respond? With the Word of God.

Look up Deuteronomy 6:16. Now read Matthew 4:7.

God is not meant to be tested. Period. There's really not much to elaborate on. Have you ever prayed one of those prayers that goes something like, "Dear God, if You get me out of this situation, I'll do whatever You want." Yeah, me too. But we need to stop it. God does not need tested, and He is not out there looking to make deals. Jesus knew this and had no desire to manipulate God by jumping off the highest point of the temple.

Temptation 3

The devil takes Him even higher now. He shows Jesus all the kingdoms of the world, offering it all to Him if Jesus simply bows and worships him. How does Jesus respond? With the Word of God!

Read Deuteronomy 6:13 and Matthew 4:10.

This is the final Word needed to end the time of temptation in the desert. Jesus proclaims that He will only serve and worship God. Period.

Did you notice that all the passages Jesus quoted during His time in the desert come from Deuteronomy? Go back and read Deuteronomy 6 and 8.

This is the last book Moses writes to the people of Israel, who have been traveling in the desert. It is a new generation of people, and he wants to make sure they don't forget what is most important—loving and honoring God. These specific chapters, the ones quoted by Jesus, go into detail about God's provision and love for them while encouraging them to reciprocate that love by showing faithfulness to God.

We are called to that same faithfulness. The laws and sacrifice no longer apply because Jesus was offered as the ultimate sacrifice, who cleansed and created a path for direct relationships with God. We are also given the Spirit, who led and empowered Jesus in the desert, to lead us and strengthen us as well. To check out all that the Spirit can do, read Galatians 5:13–22, and be encouraged that you are not alone in times of temptation and testing.

WHAT'S YOUR FAVORITE DRINK?

My kids love chocolate milk, but it's not something we always keep in the house. So there are times when they ask for chocolate milk, but all we have is plain milk, which leads to inevitable grumbling and complaining. One time Jesus was at a wedding party, and they ran out of wine. I imagine the responses of the party guests were similar to those of my kids at the breakfast table when we run out of chocolate milk.

Jesus's mom was at this party and basically told Him to take care of it. He tells the servants to fill up some water pots. There were six of them, each able to hold about twenty to thirty gallons. Do the math. That's a lot of water!

I would guess that the grumbling shifted from the party people to the servants tasked with collecting over a hundred gallons of water when what the party really needs is wine. Seriously, just imagine filling up pots with all that water. I would probably be rolling my eyes because it literally makes no sense. The guests aren't looking for water to keep the party going. Wine is what they want.

But when the water pots are full, Jesus tells them to take some of that water and give it to the master of the feast. They do as they're told, and when the drink is tasted, a celebration is held.

Wait, what? Let's check that.

> The master of the banquet tasted the water that had
> been turned into wine. (John 2:9 NIV)

It was definitely wine now, and no grapes were involved.

But not only did the water become wine, it became the best wine. By the time a party was winding down, they would usually bring out the lower-shelf variety of wine because they drank the good stuff when the party was just starting. But here they were, drinking the best wine of the night at the end of the party. And it came from a jug that had contained water only moments before. It seemed crazy to them in the moment. But what if the servants had refused to fill the water pots because it hadn't made sense to them?

I'm sure it seemed ridiculous and unnecessary to collect so much water when wine was what they needed. It just looked like water to them, but Jesus used their efforts to transform it into wine. Is there anything in your life that just looks like water right now? Something that is okay but not what you're actually hoping to have.

Maybe you're a decade into a job that was just supposed to be temporary, and you're still praying for a dream job that uses your college degree.

Maybe singleness seems to be your never-ending relationship status, but you had really hoped to be married by the time you were thirty.

Maybe your fur babies keep multiplying, but you hoped for a home filled with little giggles.

Our testing doesn't always come in the form of resisting something. There are times when we are tested by efforts that don't make sense to us but that we are willing to put into a situation. Sometimes the water pots in our lives are heavy and time consuming. But under the supervision of Jesus, our efforts are not in vain. Whatever water pots He has told us to fill have a purpose, even if it is not obvious in the moment.

Are you amid some water pots and hoping for wine?

Keep trusting. Keep filling. It will be transformed into something better than you could have ever imagined.

A COMFORTER WHO WEEPS AND KNOWS MY SORROW

Life hurts sometimes. I'm sure you don't need me to tell you that. We make mistakes, people disappoint us, plans don't work out, tragedy shows up when least expected, and complicated circumstances seem to lurk around all sorts of corners.

When life hurts, what do you do?

> Run away like Hagar?
> Slice off an ear like Peter?
> Hide like Elijah?

I've tried variations of all those options, and they usually just prolong the hurt. So may I suggest something different?

> Sit quietly like Mary.
> Praise like David.
> Sing like Paul and Silas.

God whispered to Elijah in the cave, invited Peter to breakfast on the beach, and found Hagar in the wilderness. He will always seek and comfort. He will always show up. But why do we have to make it more complicated by running, fighting, and hiding?

I think we all have our reasons. Shame, guilt, anger, and fear are probably a few good ones we come up with. But God is our Creator and Savior. He wants to love and console us through all the hurts life has to offer. He simply wants us to come and sit at His feet and offer praises, knowing that He will be with us through it all. The world is a mess because of sin, but that doesn't mean God is missing in action while we are in the middle of pain and problems.

He is with us.

He was in the desert with Hagar and in the cave with Elijah. He was with Peter on the beach and Paul in the prison. He called Lazarus out of the grave and sat at the well with a scorned woman. He showed up kneeling in the dirt and hanging on a cross. God knows pain and continues to show up when we face the damage this broken world can create. He never intended for us to know most of what we have experienced that has shattered our hearts and damaged our bodies. But we are promised that a day will come when there are no more tears and no more suffering. Until then, we have a Comforter who is always close enough to heal our wounds and soothe our souls.

God is with us, forever and always. Join me as we share our sorrows and seek God through our tears, knowing that He is there with outstretched arms.

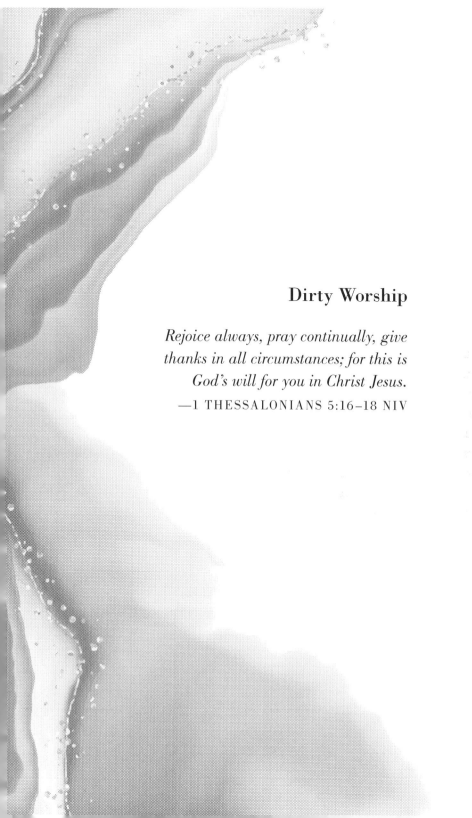

Dirty Worship

Rejoice always, pray continually, give thanks in all circumstances; for this is God's will for you in Christ Jesus.
—1 THESSALONIANS 5:16–18 NIV

WHY DO BAD THINGS HAPPEN TO GOOD PEOPLE?

Job is described as a blameless and upright man. But he battled the same thoughts many of us have and had trouble staying positive on his dark days. As Job is stripped of all that he loves, he becomes so disheveled and disgruntled that he literally starts to wonder why he was ever born.

I've never experienced what Job is described as having endured. Of course, I've had some sorrows of my own. I have had those moments that felt dark and dismal, like there was no end in sight. I'm sure you have too.

It's not quite from the place of misery loves company, but I appreciate knowing that I am not the only one who has struggled with dark times. It's honestly comforting to witness someone else having a pity party similar to the ones I often have alone in my room when nobody is watching.

But then I think about the words Job spoke to his wife shortly after the death of their children. His wife, in her understandable pain and frustration, advised Job to just curse God and die. His response to her was actually a question, one I think would benefit all of us to ponder:

> We take the good days from God, why not also the
> bad days? (Job 2:10 MSG)

Job is basically saying that if you're thanking and praising God with outstretched arms on the good days, then you should be able to do the same on the bad ones. For Job to be saying this after all he just experienced is really kind of a big deal. He literally lost all the people he loved in the blink of an eye. He was a man who did everything right but experienced what must have felt like an unbelievable kind of grief.

Unimaginable loss and pain would have hit him in an instant. So what did he do? He fell and worshipped.

He fell.

He worshipped.

Both actions are important. As believers, we sometimes think that we have to stand tall with a smile on our faces to prove our trust in God when the world is crumbling around us. But Job fell in the dirt with sorrow. And it was from that position that he chose to worship. Easier said than done though, right?

The bad days are considered bad for a reason. They carry pain and sorrow and frustration. The last thing we typically want to do is praise and pursue God in those moments. But that's exactly what we should be doing.

Why? Because God is always good, even on the bad days. Our world is broken by sin, but God is good.

The book of Job has the potential to leave us with more questions than answers. It never fully resolves the issue we all have in understanding suffering and evil, especially when it happens to people who are considered exceptionally good. As people living in a temporary world that is broken and bruised by sin, we have no choice but to sit in that tension. But we also have the privilege of knowing more than Job did at the time of his discouragement.

We know Jesus. We know He came to restore this world. It doesn't fix the temporary moments of pain, but that knowledge promises an eternity of healing, which gives us a glimmer of hope in the darkness and eases the hurt. That is why we can praise Him on the good days and on the bad ones.

Connection and Conversation

What comes to mind when you think about worship? It might be getting dressed up and going to church and singing and clapping along to the music. It might be walking through the woods and soaking in God's creation. It might be gathering around a table with friends, praying together, and sharing a meal. It might be logging on for a service to listen and soak in the Word.

Those are all great options to connect with God and praise Him through worship. But may I just offer a friendly reminder that worship isn't always pretty?

We can worship with tears in our eyes. We can worship with broken hearts. We can worship as we fall to the ground, unable to stand in our sorrows. We can worship while scared. We can worship without all the answers.

Whatever life looks like at any moment, we can worship. We learn a lot about worshipping beyond our circumstances when we look at the worship style of Daniel. If you're familiar with Daniel, then you know that he ends up in a den of lions. While that is an exciting story to talk about, and one that definitely has a grand finale worth celebrating, taking some time to read and better understand how he ended up with the lions can help us learn why worship is so important, especially in those times when it doesn't totally make sense to pray and praise.

Read Daniel 1

Daniel and his friends are being held in captivity by the king of Babylon after being exiled from Jerusalem. They were selected to be trained as part of the king's service. It is a rigorous training program that would take three years to complete, and it requires them to assimilate into the Babylonian culture. You probably noticed pretty quickly that Daniel isn't willing to do that. He refuses to eat the rich food and drink provided for them, noting that it would defile him. So he requests healthier options of fruits and vegetables. Daniel even goes as far as to challenge them to test others with his diet requests for ten days and compare it to what they were offering to see which would produce better results. What was the result? Daniel was right. The king found him and his friends to be the best in strength and wisdom. That's a pretty good start. Doesn't seem like he would be anywhere close to landing in a cave with hungry lions. But let's keep reading.

Read Daniel 2

The king needed a disturbing dream interpreted, and he calls on all his usual magicians, enchanters, sorcerers, and astrologers. But none of them can tell him the meaning of the dream, so the king orders for them to be killed. But before that happens, Daniel steps in. Now remember Daniel 1:17. God gave Daniel the ability to understand visions and dreams of all kinds. So Daniel does that for the king; he interprets the dream that has been causing a stir among everyone.

Read Daniel 2:48–49 Again

Daniel's now in a position of high power, and he brought his friends along with him. Still doesn't sound like a guy ready to be thrown into a den of angry lions. So what happens in the next chapter?

Read Daniel 3

The king makes a statue of himself and demands that everyone bow to and worship his image when they hear music. If they don't obey, he threatens that they will be thrown into a fiery furnace. Daniel's friends refuse to worship a golden idol crafted to look like the king. The king's men throw Shadrach, Meshach, and Abednego into the fire. Remember when we talked about God being a provider, and these men being willing to trust him even if they don't come out on the other side of the flames? Well, we're told that a fourth figure is visible with them in the furnace, and the three friends come out of the heat unharmed. Pretty incredible, right? Even more amazing is that they receive another promotion after this. Even though it all started with them not following the king's rules and refusing to worship anyone other than the God of Israel. They honored God in their worship and are blessed because of it against the threat of harm and what seemed like impossible odds.

After this, Daniel interprets another dream. The king goes a bit crazy and eventually dies. So a new king takes over and is even worse than the last one. He uses goblets that were stolen from the temple of Jerusalem as party glasses. And it all goes quickly downhill from there.

Daniel is again called on to interpret a dream, which ultimately leads to him being clothed in purple with a gold chain around his neck and labeled the third-highest ruler in the kingdom. Then that king dies too. So now we're on to our third king in the time Daniel has been in Babylon. He continues to become more powerful and prestigious while maintaining his devotion to God above all else. Still doesn't sound like a guy who is going to be sacrificed to the mouths of lions.

Pick Up Your Reading with Daniel 6

Many of the other people in charge are jealous at how popular Daniel has been with the kings. Think back to when we were introduced to Daniel. He was a young man brought in from a foreign land that had been conquered. After being sent to Babylon and trained as a soldier, he refused to eat their food and worship their gods. But somehow, he was almost running the place at this point. It's easy to see why they would be getting jealous. The new guy shows up with no experience, doesn't bother following the rules, and is somehow becoming employee of the month. So they come up with a plan to stop him. They convince the new king to create a law forbidding anyone from praying to a god other than him. But this time, instead of a fiery furnace, the punishment would be the lion's den. How does Daniel respond? By doing exactly what he always did.

> Now when Daniel learned the decree had been published, he went home to his upstairs room where the windows opened toward Jerusalem. Three times a day he got down on his knees and prayed, giving thanks to his God, just as he had done before. (Daniel 6:10 NIV)

Daniel's behavior does not change because of the decree. He continues to worship, and he doesn't hide it. He worships regularly, and he worships openly.

So just like his friends had been thrown into the fiery furnace, Daniel is thrown into the lions' den with a proclamation from the king with hope that he may be saved by the God he serves. He remains in the den overnight, making his own proclamation when the stone is removed from the opening. Daniel tells them that an angel had arrived to shut the mouths of the lions.

The king issues a new decree:

> For he is the living God and he endure forever; his kingdom will not be destroyed, his dominion will never end. He rescues and he saves; he performs signs and wonders in the heavens and on the earth.

He has rescued Daniel from the power of the lions.
(Daniel 6:26–27 NIV)

Daniel was a young man thrown into a pit with some lions because he refused to worship a king who was not the King. He worshipped God and was willing to be tossed into an impossible situation to honor that relationship. His worship was a personal practice of devotion to God, but it had an impact on all those who saw the faith of this man and the presence of his living God.

Worship saved his life and changed the lives of those who saw God's power on display.

Life can get complicated sometimes; it can feel nearly impossible to survive. But we have examples like Daniel who remind us that God can shut the mouths of lions and preserve us in the darkest places imaginable when we have enough faith to trust Him.

If you find yourself somewhere that feels like a deep and dark den of lions, channel your inner Daniel as you choose to pray and praise in those moments rather than worry and wonder. Choose to honor the King, and trust that God will deliver you through it all, even if it seems impossible.

HAVE YOU EVER FELT TRAPPED?

If you have lived in the unprecedented times we first experienced in 2020, you have probably been like me and caught yourself thinking more than once, *I can't do this again.* Especially while working in health care, it has been a continuous, vicious cycle of restrictions and rules that are exhausting, confusing, and scary. But amid those thoughts, I've been learning from a couple guys named Paul and Silas. They had been going around teaching about Jesus, which led to an unexpected church service one night in an unlikely location:

> Around midnight Paul and Silas were praying and
> singing hymns to God, and the other prisoners were
> listening to them. (Acts 16:25 NIV)

Yes, Paul and Silas were prisoners, which means they were leading this impromptu church service while locked in a prison cell. I've been stuck in traffic and found it easy to complain, but these guys were in prison and praising. If that's not crazy enough, an earthquake hit, and the prison doors opened.

But did they leave? Nope. They stayed in prison after the doors flew open.

Wasn't freedom what they were praying about? Nope. They already had freedom, and it had nothing to do with the doors of this prison. Paul says it like this: "Now the Lord is the Spirit, and where the Spirit of the Lord is, there is freedom" (2 Corinthians 3:17 NIV).

Paul and Silas weren't praising God in hopes that He would grant them freedom from this prison cell. Paul and Silas were praising *with* God in that prison cell. That's a big difference. They knew God was with them, and that was enough reason to worship.

That wasn't their first experience with chains. I'm sure it would have been easy for them to think, *I can't do this again*, when they heard the heavy doors of the prison close. But they had the strength to do it again and to praise in the prison because they knew God was there with them through the Spirit.

Our chains and prisons come in all shapes and sizes. They might be financial debt, illness, mental health issues, difficult relationships. Add in a global pandemic that never seems to end, racial tensions, and political disputes. The chains can be very heavy, and the prison walls can be daunting. But what if you knew that you weren't alone?

The truth is that the shackles might fall off, but they also might not. But when you are able to lift up praises with God, it honestly won't matter if the doors fly open or if they stay closed. It won't matter if you get out of debt or file bankruptcy. It won't matter if the diagnosis is terminal or temporary. It won't matter if the relationship ends or is restored. Don't stop praying and hoping that the doors will be opened and the chains broken. But start praising before any of that happens simply because the presence of God is with you through it all.

Paul and Silas stayed in the prison after the doors were opened because they wanted others to know the presence of God. They had already found freedom that went beyond their cell and wanted to make sure others could experience it too. By staying, they showed those around them a freedom that goes beyond the shackles.

Rather than feeling trapped in a prison, celebrate true release, and use the shackles in your life to show others what real freedom is all about.

The Snuggle Is Real

*Draw near to God, and He
will draw near to you.*
—JAMES 4:8A NIV

ARE YOU A MORNING BIRD OR A NIGHT OWL?

I struggle with sleep. I often wake up at 3 a.m., my mind twisting and spiraling. I worry. I plan. I think. I prepare. But what I really need to do is just sleep.

Peter was someone who figured out how to sleep, and he has taught me a few things.

The church was being assembled after Jesus rose from the dead and went into heaven. The Spirit was sent to believers, and they were doing pretty well. Peter was preaching to thousands of people at a time, healing people, and casting out demons. But all that got him was some unwanted attention.

He ended up in prison amid Christians being executed. It appeared that his name was next on the list. The night before he was to be brought out for execution, an angel woke him. He had been sound sleep, chained between two guards. Read that again. Peter was awaiting his execution, and the angel had to wake him up. He was sleeping while awaiting a gruesome death sentence.

The slightest inconvenience in life will keep me up at night. The most ridiculous and unrealistic scenario will have me tossing and turning. But here's Peter, getting some shut-eye instead of anxiously awaiting his inevitably painful death. How? I have to think it's because he learned from the best.

Back when Jesus was walking this earth, Peter was one of the chosen disciples who got to walk with Him. After a long day, Jesus took them out in a boat to head across a lake. A storm began to rage, terrifying the disciples. Meanwhile, where was Jesus? Sleeping.

Jesus woke up, frustrated by their fear, and calmed the storm. He asked the disciples, "Where is your faith?"

Fast-forward to Peter, sleeping in his prison cell, shackled and surrounded, awaiting execution. How could he sleep with all that was raging around him? Easy. Peter found the answer to the question Jesus asked the disciples on the boat. He found his faith. He discovered the peace available to us when we trust God beyond our temporary circumstances.

Peter went from shouting from panic in a storm to sleeping through a death sentence in a prison cell. By being close to Jesus, he learned about the peace that comes from knowing God can calm the storm and unlock the prison cells. He also knew that even if the storm raged and the doors stayed locked, faith would lead him into an eternal peace. That sounds like a win-win situation.

So if life feels like a storm or you woke up today trapped in what seems like a prison cell, get closer to God, and go to sleep. Find your faith. Discover His peace.

Connection and Conversation

Let's dig a little deeper into this idea of sleeping through the storms and what Jesus taught about true rest. But before we get started, think about what keeps you up at night. Write it down.

Read Matthew 8:23–27

Jesus tucked himself in and laid down for a nap after a long day of teaching with His disciples. They went out for a boat ride to get away from the crowds. But as Jesus snuggled up with a pillow and blanket, a fierce storm started raging around them. Their boat began to fill with water as they were tossed around on the lake.

"Do you not care that we're perishing?" the disciples asked in a panic as they woke Him. The panicked disciples felt like Jesus was sleeping through the storm, leaving them to die. Have you ever felt like that? Fighting with a family member, unexpected illness, addiction, not enough in your bank account to pay the bills, death, loneliness, job loss, anxiety. The list of storms in life can be fierce and overwhelming. It's easy to feel like God is sleeping through our storms when the waves don't stop crashing against us. It's normal to feel alone and think that you need to somehow get God's attention when you can't see anything beyond the storm. Our prayers can end up sounding like the desperate pleas of the disciples, thinking that God is unavailable when we really need Him.

"Where is your faith?" Jesus asked as He woke up and calmed the storm.

They woke Him up for help, but Jesus wanted them to have enough faith to rest with Him and to trust the storm wasn't going to destroy them. Instead of thinking that we need to wake Him up, God wants us to know that He is already in control of all the storms. We can simply rest in His presence, finding a peace that calms all storms. Let's learn more about this peaceful rest.

Read Matthew 11:28–30

"Come to me, and I will give you rest." That's the promise. Go to God and receive rest. But how does that work exactly? It means when we come to Jesus, all our problems will be solved, and life will be easy. Right? Nope!

The rest He promises doesn't come from all our problems going away. The illness doesn't always heal. The relationship doesn't always work out. The bills don't always get paid. Life delivers a lot of burdens along the way, and they can become very heavy. Some of these burdens are the ones we pick up ourselves based on choices we have made. Others have been placed on our shoulders, and we can't seem to shrug them off no matter how hard we try.

Well, Jesus gives us some further instructions on what happens when we come to Him with a heavy load.

Jesus said, "Take my yoke upon you."

Wait, what?

A yoke is a wooden beam that connects two animals so they can work together to carry a load. But if I'm already weighed down with my own burdens, why would I be looking to share anyone else's yoke? I showed up for the promise of rest, not more work. But the simple answer is that Jesus's yoke is different. It's easy. It means that He carries the weight and guides us through, literally side by side with us. This isn't the first time He has carried something for us.

Read 1 Peter 2:24

Jesus carried the weight of the world on His shoulders when He went to the cross, bearing all our sins on His own. The heaviness of our sins was transformed into the freedom of salvation. He's already done the heavy lifting, and He's offering to continue carrying our burdens. Give Him what is heavy, and He'll give you what is light. Go to Him with all your burdens, and He will give you rest.

He can handle whatever you are carrying that feels too heavy for you. He's already done it. He is simply asking that you take on the light yoke of believing in Him enough to trust Him with the complications of life.

HAVE YOU EVER NOTICED THAT KIDS LIVE DIFFERENTLY THAN WE DO?

I recently scolded one of my girls for being careless as she rummaged through a basket of clean clothes and threw them on the floor. But after I gathered up the clothes, I had to wonder if she was really being careless.

Kids are special little beings. They are dependent on the grown-ups in their lives but love to try new things. They live in the moment, rarely worrying about the future. They trust quickly, learn constantly, and apologize easily. I don't think kids are actually capable of being careless. Rather, they are designed to be beautifully carefree.

Being careless implies you neglected something that was your responsibility. To be carefree means living as though that burden was never given to you in the first place. Doesn't it sound amazing to be carefree like a child?

Jesus told His disciples that they needed to be more like kids. Their carefree nature is what God wants from us in our relationships with Him. He wants us to live with childlike joy, not judgment. He wants us to love deeply and seek the comfort of our Father. He wants us to live with the peace that comes from knowing it's not all up to us.

But as we get older, that gets hard as we take on more responsibilities. It feels unrealistic to live with an open heart after we've been hurt. We struggle with releasing control as there is more to lose if it all goes wrong. Being carefree starts to seem impossible.

But Peter tells us that it is because of who God is that we can enjoy the freedom of being carefree with Him and live with a childlike faith: "Live carefree before God, because He is most careful with you" (1 Peter 5:7 MSG).

We can live without worry and fear because God is the careful one. He holds our futures and wants all that is good for every one of us. He will carefully guide us through the challenges of this broken world if we let Him.

Fulfill your obligations, and teach your children responsibility. Those things are still important. But stop living as though the burdens of this life are all on your shoulders and yours alone. Take a deep breath, and enjoy His beauty surrounding you today, carefree like a child in the presence of a loving parent. One that won't even scold you for sometimes making a little mess.

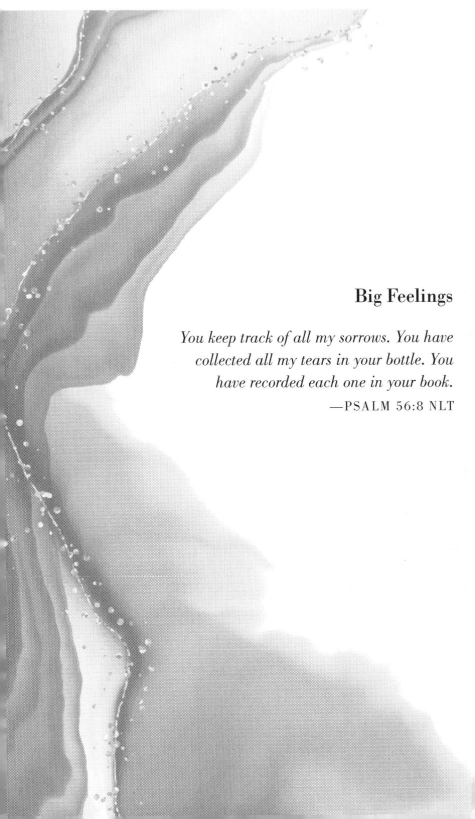

Big Feelings

*You keep track of all my sorrows. You have
collected all my tears in your bottle. You
have recorded each one in your book.*

—PSALM 56:8 NLT

ANYONE ELSE ALWAYS OFFERING TO HOLD A BABY?

I love babies. I really love brand-new babies, the ones who just want to snuggle up and be held. They're just so peaceful in a way that's almost contagious. They offer me a kind of peace that I can't seem to conjure up on my own most days.

I am usually a whirlwind of anxiety. I don't sleep well and drink too much coffee, ending up tense and tired. But all of that disappears when I'm holding a baby.

What if that feeling could last? What if there is peace available that started a long time ago with a snuggly little baby?

Way before this particular baby was born, prophets spoke of His birth and proclaimed that He would be the one to bring peace to all nations. Not just any kind of peace, but the kind that can fully restore us with wholeness and tranquility. God's people understood this peace. You can find it scattered throughout their original scriptures, referring to it as shalom as they share about God's provision and peace in their lives. But that peace became more than just an understanding when it became tangible, coming in the form of a tiny baby who grew into the man we know as Jesus.

When He was preparing for His return to heaven, Jesus had a few conversations with His closest friends. Jesus told them they would experience pain, sorrow, grief, and suffering. But He also encouraged them all of that would turn into joy, and they would be able to rejoice again in His presence.

> I have told you these things, so that in me you may
> have peace. In this world you will have trouble.

But take heart! I have overcome the world. (John 16:33 NIV)

This world is going to give you trouble sometimes. That's a guarantee straight from Jesus. But Jesus overcame all those troubles. That's also a guarantee.

It doesn't mean that all our troubles immediately disappear. But it does means that even while in the midst of them, we have a peace that goes beyond our understanding and is more powerful than any problem.

So how do we get that peace without being able to actually snuggle this peaceful baby? Luckily, Jesus left us with His peace. The power that was used to overcome the troubles of the world now dwells within us, flowing through us during the sorrows and strains of life as the Spirit of God, our Comforter.

I'm going to keep snuggling all the babies I can. But I'm also learning that the peace I really need has already been given to me by a tiny baby who changed the world.

Connection and Conversation

It was a July weekend a few years ago when I found out I was pregnant by experiencing a miscarriage. In terms of medical intervention required, it was pretty mild, so I barely told anyone. But when I lost the chance to feel my baby growing in my belly and snuggling in my arms, I was a mess of emotions on the inside. I felt overwhelming sadness. But I also got really mad.

I was mad at God.

Without getting into weird specifics, this was my last chance to have another baby. So the thought that kept resonating in my mind was, *Why bother introducing me in that moment of miscarriage to this little life I was never going to keep?* The question just kept rolling around in my mind, angrily demanding an answer from God.

If I'm honest, this was the only conversation I had with Him for about a year. And to be really honest, I never got an answer. But I'm also not angry anymore. God and I figured some things out together during those frustrated conversations. If you've ever felt angry at God, I'd like to walk you through some of our conversation topics in the hope you can find a way to talk with Him about it too.

Read 1 Peter 5:7

It's a simple statement written in a letter by Peter that says we can cast all our cares on God because He cares for us. Well, what about when it feels like He doesn't care?

I felt so alone, and God felt so far away from me. It was hard for me to cast all my cares on and talk to God about my anger because it just felt like if He cared, it never would have happened.

Then I spent some time with Hagar. Remember her? She was the servant who had a baby with Abraham when he was being impatient about God's promises.

Read Genesis 16

Abraham and his wife, Sarah, were having trouble conceiving and were impatient. So Abraham had a baby with Hagar. But she panicked and ran into the desert. God met her there in her distress, and she identified Him as "the God who sees me." She felt seen by God in the desert of her scared sorrow. So she returned, comforted by the presence of God.

Read Genesis 21:8–20

But then Sarah got jealous. Hagar was kicked out into the desert with her baby, alone and prepared for them both to die. But the angel of God showed up and cared for her in the desert. This time, opening her eyes to see a well of water to sustain them.

God showed up and saw the distress Hagar was experiencing. He was with her and a source of comfort during the unknown circumstances. God showed up again and helped her to see His provision when she found herself in the desert again with even more distress and unknown circumstances. God saw her and helped her to see what was still available to her when all hope seemed lost.

I started to remind myself of this in those moments when I felt really alone and unseen, lost in the thoughts of a future with no hope. The anger was still there though. Then a friend reminded me that God cries too.

Read John 11:1–43

Jesus showed up at the tomb of one of his dearest friends, who had been dead for days at that point. He encountered Lazarus's sisters at the tomb. He was confronted by their frustration that He had arrived too late and by their hope that something could still be done. He stood and wept with them. Literally, Jesus wept.

The reasons for His tears can be debated, but as I read that verse with my own broken heart, I was assured by those simple words that Jesus shares in our human experiences of loss. God shares in the intricacies of our hearts, thoughts, and emotions. He wept at the tomb of His friend, and He weeps with us in our losses too.

But in my anger, I made Him my adversary. I blamed Him for the sorrow and had never allowed God close enough to grieve with me. With that realization, I was finally able to be honest with God about my anger and let Him close enough to do something about it. I stopped accusing and started inviting Him into the anger, recognizing that He knows my pain and wants to stand at the entrance to the tomb and weep with me.

Whatever it is that is causing you pain, He is weeping with you too. For now, at least.

Read Revelation 21:1–4

John received the revelation of what would come in the future and describes a new heaven and a new earth that will be different from what we now know and understand. He tells us that there will be no more sorrow and no more death. But the verse I can't help but visualize and cling to in my sorrow is this: "He will wipe every tear from their eyes" (Revelation 21:4a NIV).

He showed up in the desert with Hagar and provided for her. He showed up at the tomb and wept with the sisters of Lazarus. He is preparing a place for us, where we will be greeted by His promises and a loving embrace as He wipes away our tears because there will be no need for them in His glory.

He sees you. He weeps with you. He is preparing a place of complete healing for you. He is our Comforter.

HAVE YOU EVER FELT HEAVY?

I'm not talking about the number on the scale. I'm talking about a heaviness inside that can't be seen but shows up in other ways. For example, through:

- Exhaustion
- Sadness
- Isolation
- Fear
- Hopelessness
- Frustration
- Weariness

It's a deep heaviness, kind of like when you get a chill but can't seem to warm up. There's a passage in Isaiah where the prophet talks about this spirit of heaviness and offers something for it. The prophet, on behalf of God, says there is something we should wrap ourselves up in when experiencing this kind of heaviness.

I don't know about you, but there is nothing I love more than snuggling up under a fuzzy blanket when the air gets chilly. It's cozy and comfortable, which is exactly what I need. That's the kind of feeling Isaiah is offering for our heaviness. He's not exactly recommending a fuzzy blanket, but he is suggesting a garment of praise.

But why praise? That's often one of the last things I reach for when life is going wrong, and I'm feeling heavy inside. But Isaiah—and a lot of other people in the Bible we've already talked about—tell us that it's the most cozy and comfortable option, especially when sorrow or sickness become heavy. When we wrap up in praise, we are actually rejoicing in hope.

Praise doesn't fix our problems right away, but it gives us hope. That hope gives us a warm and fuzzy feeling that relieves the heaviness as it wraps us up in His grace. While we are snuggled up in praise, we are steadily reminded of all that God has offered and promised. His promises provide for the moment and extend beyond current circumstances.

So if you are feeling heavy today, find some praise, and snuggle up with it for a while. It's time to get cozy and rejoice.

A SAVIOR WHO OFFERS GRACE AS A LOVING EMBRACE

I always feel nervous when waiting in line at the TSA. There's this anxious energy as I wait and wonder if I'll make it through the line without issues. It's not like I'm smuggling anything illegal in my bags, but I still feel like there's a chance I'm not going to make it through. Like maybe I got something wrong when I was packing.

If I'm being honest, that's often how I've pictured standing at the pearly gates. Waiting in line, fidgeting back and forth, nervously looking around, and anxiously messing with whatever I can find in my pockets.

Wondering if something is going to be found that stops me from going through to my destination.

Worried that God is going to find something I wasn't meant to bring with me and turn me away.

Thinking about all the moments and missteps I've hidden away.

I've lived most of my life trying to be good enough so that God would reserve my spot for me in eternity. Always trying my best to pack the right bag for the destination.

Sure, I'd mess up, but I always asked for forgiveness and tried to repack my bag the best I could. Praying I did it right this time.

This process is exhausting and has made me unsure about how to approach God now, before I've even had a chance to step up to the gates. But I'm learning that we shouldn't be nervous or worried about what we're carrying with us and what He might find when taking a look.

The author of Hebrews tells us to come boldly to the throne of our gracious God. Promising that it is in His presence where we will receive His mercy and the grace to help us when we need it most. Instead of worrying about what He is going to find, look forward to what we will find with Him.

God already knows about your baggage. He knows what you've buried deep and hidden behind something else, hoping that it wouldn't be found. He knows what you forgot to pack or what you have tried to forget was still in there.

He wants to find what is hidden, not so He can punish or banish, but so that He can offer grace. The kind of grace that packs the bag and books the ticket.

There's no need to stand in line anxious and worried anymore. Join me as we approach Him boldly, so we can get on with the adventures He has planned for us.

Lost and Found

*For the Son of Man came to
seek and to save the lost.*
—LUKE 19:10 NIV

HAVE YOU EVER LOST ANYTHING REALLY IMPORTANT?

Something terrible happened this weekend.

I put together an entire puzzle, except for one missing piece. Okay, maybe describing it as terrible is a little dramatic, but if you have ever put together a brand-new puzzle and found yourself one piece, you understand the feeling!

I was tempted to forget about that missing piece and just start a new puzzle. But there was no way that was going to happen. The puzzle would stay out until the piece was found. I was determined. Well, I'm happy to report that the missing piece was found during a massive clean and search party.

I left the 299 and found the 1.

Finding that puzzle piece gave me a taste of the feeling described in the parable Jesus told of the shepherd finding his lost sheep.

He left the ninety-nine and found the one.

Jesus described the shepherd as picking up the sheep and going back to celebrate, calling everyone to join him. While I can compare this parable to the excitement of finding my missing puzzle piece and calling my kids to celebrate with me, Jesus actually compares these sheep to us. He tells those listening that the heavens rejoice when someone who wanders is found.

Why is it so exciting?

Thinking of the puzzle, each piece is perfectly unique and important. Without every piece, the picture is incomplete. But as one of the pieces, sometimes it's hard to see that.

God always sees the whole picture. In fact, He was the one who created the picture in the beginning and the one who works it to completion. He looks at the ninety-nine with love as they are connected to each other, intricately woven together. He also looks at the open space, knowing exactly who belongs there and longing for them.

If we're the sheep, He's the shepherd.

We're told in the Twenty-Third Psalm all the ways the shepherd cares for us. We're also told that He relentlessly pursues us with His goodness and mercy. It's literally impossible for us to wander too far to be out of His sight and His plan for us.

If you're the one, and He wants to bring you to the place He has prepared for you.

If you're the ninety-nine, enjoy the connection, and get ready to celebrate!

Connection and Conversation

As a kid, I was taught to count sheep as a way to fall asleep. But now that I'm an adult with reckless thoughts swirling around my mind, especially at night, counting sheep doesn't usually work. Instead, I've learned that I should be talking to the shepherd instead of trying to simply count His sheep. There is a familiar passage that references the shepherd. One who provides for all our needs, guides us to places for peaceful rest, and restores the depths of our souls. A guide who is with us in the darkness of death and sits with us in the presence of our enemies. I remember being taught to memorize this passage as a child, and I have since recited it countless times seated at the bedside of someone approaching the end of his or her life. I now use it as a prayer many nights to calm my turbulent mind. So let's take some time to go through it, understand a bit more about who wrote it, and figure out how to really talk to our shepherd.

Read Psalm 23

What needs are being addressed by the shepherd? What promises do you notice being offered as you read through this passage?

This psalm is packed with fear and frustration, anxiousness, wandering, and weariness. It is also filled with rest and restoration, course correction, pursuit, and peace.

It was written by someone who understood shame, fear, anxiety, and failure. It was written by someone who also understood God's abundant grace, mercy, goodness, and love. It was written by David.

Read 1 Samuel 16:1–13

Samuel is a prophet of God, tasked with anointing the king of Israel. This is the second time he has done this; the first time was with Saul. Remember when Samuel found him looking for the donkeys? If you need a refresher, you can read about him in 1 Samuel 8–15. The people of Israel felt like they really needed a king to keep things in order. God wanted them to recognize that He was enough for them but sent Samuel to anoint a king for them. Saul did okay at first. But he ended up not being obedient to what God called him to do. So Samuel was sent out in search of another king to anoint on God's behalf. If you read that passage in 1 Samuel 16, you'll see that David was selected and anointed. But did you notice where David was called in from for the anointing? He was shepherding the flock.

Read 1 Samuel 16:14–23

Although David received the anointing from God to be king, Saul still held the role. He was experiencing a deep darkness now that his connection with God had changed, and he needed someone to soothe him. Someone thought David could help. He was known to have musical talent and the Spirit of God. So they sent for him. But did you notice where David was called in from to serve the king? He was shepherding the flock.

Read 1 Samuel 17

David and Goliath. If you grew up in church, you have heard of the unlikely young man with a stone and a sling who conquered the giant. It's an incredible testimony to God's provision and protection. Everyone was fearful and couldn't defeat the enemy before them. Then David showed up without armor and minimal weaponry. But did you notice where David was called in from for battle? He was shepherding the flock.

So we know that David is a shepherd who has been told that God wants him to be king. He knows what it is like to care for a flock, provide for their needs, protect them from harm, and remain with them. He also knows that God has made some big promises.

Read 1 Samuel 18:1–16 and 1 Samuel 19:1–18

Things take a turn for David as Saul becomes fueled by jealousy and seeks to have him killed. Their volatile relationship continues for a few more chapters as Saul pursues David. But David is continually delivered through the help of faithful friends and God's provision and plan for his life.

Read 1 Samuel 24 and 26

David had a vicious enemy in Saul. He was hunted by Saul, who had nothing but ill intentions. And yet, when David encountered Saul in vulnerable positions and had the opportunity to end the personal battle, he didn't. He understood what it meant to have enemies. But he also trusted God enough to leave the choice of punishment or pardon to Him.

Read 2 Samuel 2:1–7, 2 Samuel 5:1–5, and 2 Samuel 7

A lot happens for David after the death of Saul. He becomes the king of Judah, defeats another king, and moves into position as king of Israel. Right where God told him he would be. But then it gets even better. David is blessed by a covenant with God that establishes him as one called to lead God's people and that his lineage would be eternally blessed. Everything is going to be great now, right? Definitely not.

Read 2 Samuel 11 and 12

Oh, David. He sets his sights on a married woman, panics when she gets pregnant, and sends her husband into battle to be murdered.

Doesn't exactly sound like a man anointed to carry the holy lineage for all eternity. Well, God wasn't pleased with him either, and there were some deeply painful consequences. But there were also renewed blessings in the birth of Solomon and God's favor in battle.

David understood what it was like to experience shame and disgust as a result of serious missteps and failures. He also understood doubting that God's blessings would remain. He experienced hopelessness and sorrow. He also experienced blessings that were unearned and grace that was not deserved.

Read 2 Samuel 22

There were years of exile, and battles raged with the people of Israel when David was their king. He never became a perfect man, but he did seek God. We see that clearly in what is described as his song of deliverance and some of his final words. He speaks of God's deliverance and praised Him for the many blessings over the course of his lifetime.

It's unclear when the Twenty-Third Psalm was written, but it feels like it could have been written toward the end of David's life, when he was reflecting on all that God had provided and protected him through. A shepherd calling out to *the* shepherd. One who had felt fear and experienced the calm God can provide. One who had enemies and had also known God's protection. One who sought the calm of pastures and still waters as battles raged. One who understood the guidance and correction of the rod and staff as he strayed and wandered. One who had been pursued by God when he could have easily been written off as someone who had gone too far.

As someone who can find a reason to worry about most things in life and has done my fair share of wandering, these promises and plans of God bring with them a lot of peace. If you find yourself feeling all the feels of David and wondering what to do with them, I'd like to share with you how I talk to the shepherd through the Twenty-Third Psalm and invite you to join me in this prayer:

Dear Lord,

With You, everything has already been given to me that I could ever need. Thank You for being my guide and my provider. Thank You for protecting and comforting me.

My mind is anxious, and my body is tense. Please lead me to a place where I can lie down in peace and experience the calm of still waters.

Will You help me to find real rest tonight and set me on the right path in the morning?

I am wandering aimlessly and am afraid that I can't find the way back on my own. The path has been dark lately. But I won't be afraid anymore. I trust You to lead me.

Help me to remember the times when You have provided support and love, times when my life has literally overflowed with blessings.

You have pursued me with Your goodness and Your mercy. Thank You for never giving up on me, my Savior and my friend.

Amen.

WANNA TALK ABOUT CIRCUMCISION?

Before you get too uncomfortable, I'm not going to give a detailed explanation of the procedure experienced by baby boys. You can google that. But I do want to talk about why it was so important in the Bible and what it still means for our lives, girls included.

The original circumcision was an act of removal intended to be a sign of promise and blessing between God and His people. Now that we live in a new promise through the sacrifice of Jesus, it's a little different. True circumcision is not something visible in the flesh. Paul told us that in his letter to the Romans. He told them circumcision of the heart, through the Spirit, is required.

But this idea of having a heart circumcision isn't some new idea that Paul created. When the Israelites were roaming in the desert and Moses was receiving direction from God, he told the people they needed to make some changes. As part of those instructions, he also mentioned a new understanding about circumcision: "Circumcise your heart and don't be stubborn anymore" (Deuteronomy 10:16 MEV).

Circumcision is an act of removal. Nobody knew this better than the Israelites. But now they were also being told to circumcise their hearts. So to have your heart circumcised must also require the removal of something. Where our hearts are concerned, it's about removing something deep. It's about removing sin. But even more than that, it's about removing the actual desire for sin from our hearts.

Think about what would change if the deep desire for sin was removed from your innermost being. In a lot of ways, life would be so much easier if certain thoughts, desires, and temptations were removed. God offers us that option, so why are we stubborn?

I would imagine if a grown man were anticipating a physical circumcision, he would be scared at the thought. I doubt you could convince many of them that it was worth it. Removing something is often painful. And sacrifice is involved, especially when we're going deep into the heart. It usually involves making some changes with the people, places, habits, and things that have become very comfortable.

So why do it?

A circumcision of the heart removes with precision what has created barriers between us and God. We're disconnected and incomplete without the procedure. Connection and the experience of being whole in the presence of your Savior is worth the uncomfortable moments of removal.

Take a deeper look, get a little uncomfortable, and remove what needs to be gone for you to be made whole.

Smelly Sacrifice

As the goat goes into the wilderness,
it will carry all the people's sins upon
itself into a desolate land.
—ROMANS 12:1 NIV

DO YOU KNOW HOW TO BUILD A CAMPFIRE?

My kids love making s'mores by the campfire. There is just something magical about watching the marshmallow toast and soften into this gooey treat. Fire is really amazing. We all know it can heat, it can cook, and it can even destroy. But did you know it can also be used to purify? When fire is used in a specific way with gold, for example, it brings the impurities to the surface, where they can be more easily removed.

God used fire to purify too. His people had guidelines for using fire as a means of purification for themselves. If you want to check out the book of Leviticus, it includes detailed instructions for animal sacrifice on an altar of fire. This practice was offered as a way to acknowledge impurities and be a substitute for their sins.

So they sacrificed many animals. But God didn't just want His people to be great at building a campfire and grilling meat. Actually, if it were up to Him, these specific sacrifices wouldn't have been needed at all.

> Do you think all God wants are sacrifices—empty rituals just for show? He wants you to listen to him! (1 Samuel 15:22 MSG)

God doesn't desire sacrifice. What He really craves from us is obedience. But we're not good at obedience. Adam and Eve proved that right from the start, when they couldn't obey the simple instruction to not eat from a specific tree. So God took matters into His own hands and offered the ultimate sacrifice. One who could be fully obedient.

And being found in appearance as a man, he humbled himself by becoming obedient to death— even death on a cross! (Philippians 2:8 NIV)

That's Jesus.

This sacrifice offered a permanent removal option for our impurities. They were all carried on the cross, and we are cleansed through the grace offered in and through His sacrifice. The practice of animal sacrifice was no longer needed. But God wasn't done with fire.

We still needed it.

When Jesus returned to the heavens, the Spirit was poured out like tongues of fire on believers. It's not a visible fire for us, but the benefits of the Spirit are still to be enjoyed by all believers. The Spirit identifies and removes our human impurities by pulling them to the surface and wiping them away with grace. We are revealed as treasured beings created in the image of a perfect Savior and prepared for humble obedience.

Connection and Conversation

Think about your favorite smell. Mine would have to be the tiny little country fair where I grew up. Sure, there are farm animals and barn odors that aren't especially pleasant. But there are also the smells of funnel cakes, french fries, and cotton candy. It is also a blend of moments and people I can't find anywhere else. Fragrances are powerful that way. With the slightest whiff they can evoke emotions, thoughts, and memories.

Do you know what smells good to God? Sacrifice. I know that sounds a little gross, but don't run away yet. Let me explain.

In the book of Leviticus, there are sixteen mentions of a pleasing aroma to God. In all those instances, the aroma is part of a sacrifice. Typically animal sacrifice, but sometimes other types of offerings. It is a daunting book, and one that I admittedly skip over often because it seems irrelevant and a little crazy. But take some time and read through Leviticus 1–7. Moses fills us in on all types of offerings, when they are used, and why they are needed. These laws of sacrifice seem insignificant to us, but they were a necessary building block of faith as they established guidelines for sin and reconciliation.

But what made this practice of sacrifice such an enjoyable smell for God?

It wasn't that He loved the scent of freshly grilled meat. It was what the sacrifice meant that made it appealing to Him. The act of sacrifice was a sign of obedience and an opportunity for people to recognize their sins and seek atonement. But it wasn't enough—not forever and not for everyone.

God knew that, so He sent Jesus.

Jesus's love for us and the sacrifice that came out of that love was a fragrant offering. The aroma of animal sacrifices was no longer needed to satisfy God and atone for our sins. It never completed the job anyway. Jesus did that as the ultimate sacrifice because it was an offering based in pure love. All those sacrificial laws you read about in Leviticus would ultimately be fulfilled in Jesus. But even though we don't have to be butchers and grill masters to worship God, we are still called to participate.

> Therefore be imitators of God as beloved children.
> Walk in love, as Christ loved us and gave Himself
> for us as a fragrant offering and a sacrifice to God.
> (Ephesians 5:2 MEV)

We were told in the beginning that we are created in God's image, and now Paul is emphasizing that we are to be imitators of God, just like a child would imitate his or her parents. In another letter, Paul tells us that we should smell like Jesus. Not literally, of course. But he says that we are to share the knowledge of Christ like a sweet perfume. We become His fragrance. Check out what Paul has to say about this in 2 Corinthians 2:14–17.

People experience this type of scent through our words, actions, and interactions. According to Paul, a whiff of us should evoke emotions, thoughts, and memories of Jesus.

Here's where it gets a little complicated. If you and I wore the same perfume, it would smell different on each of us. Hormones, pH levels, and skin types change the scent. I could also wear the same perfume all the time, and it would be perceived in different ways by various people. Some would love it; others may wish I'd used something different that day.

Fragrances are powerful that way. They transform on the person wearing them and received by others in different ways. God's fragrance is similar. We each experience the scent of Jesus differently because we are all His unique creations. Others also perceive this scent differently because they have various experiences, preferences, and understandings.

So, how do we make sure our aromas are pleasing to God and others? Paul asked that same question, recognizing that none of us are adequate to perform such a task as smelling like the sweet scent of Jesus all the time. But Paul also gave us an answer. He said that we speak in the power of Christ and in the sight of God. Basically, we must rely on the power of God to give us an extra spritz of perfume, and He delights in that scent as we share Him with others. Because when we smell like Jesus, we live like Him too. More important, we love like Him.

Jesus ate meals with tax collectors and prostitutes.

Jesus gathered up kids to sit on His lap.

Jesus healed people who hadn't been seen or touched in years.

Jesus approached the outcasts.

Jesus offered forgiveness for sins. All sins.

We are forgiven. Jesus took care of that. Now it's our turn to check our scents and make sure that they resemble the example of love He set.

HAVE YOU EVER BEEN PUNISHED?

There was one time as a kid when I got a little creative with a pen on my mom's wooden desk. Once I completed my project, I paused for a moment to appreciate it. The panic set in as I realized the damage done. I did the only thing I knew to do in that moment. I carved my sister's name into the desk like the signature of an artist on a masterpiece. I was scared of the punishment that was on its way and needed someone else to take the blame.

I needed a scapegoat.

Humans mess up a lot. God knew this and created the idea of having a scapegoat. He told the Israelites to take a goat once a year, have the priest place his hands on this goat, and tell it all the sins of the people. Once this designated animal embodied their sins, it was sent out into the wilderness.

> As the goat goes into the wilderness, it will carry
> all the people's sins upon itself into a desolate land.
> (Leviticus 16:22 NLT)

Doesn't that sound perfect, having all your sins just carried off into the middle of nowhere, never to be seen or heard from again?

That's literally grace. No goat required.

There's no need to send a goat into the wilderness anymore because God sent Jesus to embody those sins on the cross and remove them once and for all. We don't have to carve a name beneath the sins and stumbles of our lives, trying to place the blame on someone else. God already signed a name in blood. It's Jesus.

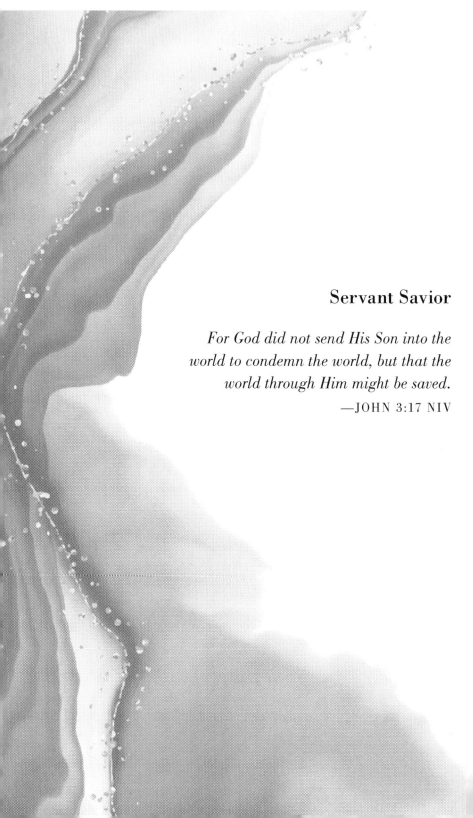

Servant Savior

For God did not send His Son into the world to condemn the world, but that the world through Him might be saved.

—JOHN 3:17 NIV

EVER SPILL COFFEE?

This week I was on my way to work and dumped a cup of coffee right down the front of my white T-shirt. I'd like to say that was the first time, but I rarely make it through a day without a stain showing up somewhere. But this one was bad. The only option was to turn my shirt around and wear it backward for the day, hiding the stains underneath my hair. A quick fix to a messy problem.

That's life, right? Things get messy. We make poor choices and screw things up in all sorts of ways. We're humans, and it's kind of always been our thing.

If you've made it this far, then you've heard about the Israelites and know they were rescued from Egypt. And after some ups and downs with mountains and deserts, a group of their descendants made it into the Promised Land. They were living it up in the fulfilled promise of God. But that wasn't enough for them.

About seven hundred years later, disagreement broke apart this nation. They were worshipping idols and not really worshipping God anymore. So a prophet named Isaiah showed up in Judah to remind them of a few things and give them some advice. He told them to wash until they were clean and to stop doing wrong. Back in the day of the Israelites, they would have talked about getting clean a lot because they had washing rituals and sacrificial practices for the cleansing of their sins.

But Isaiah goes on to say something that might have been a bit confusing for them. He said our sins were red but would be made white, like wool.

Fast-forward about another seven hundred years. There's another prophet proclaiming a message from God. John the Baptist shouted in the desert, "Look, the Lamb of God, who takes away the sin of the world!"

He saw Jesus and identified Him as the Lamb. The precious white Lamb.

God has always wanted us to be clean. He wants the marks of sin removed.

Before Jesus, they had ritual cleaning practices that removed the burdens of sin, but it ended up just being like turning their shirts around and hiding the stains for a bit. Not fully clean.

Then there was Jesus. He shed His own blood as an opportunity for us to be pure and clean in a way that wasn't possible before.

From red to white, just like Isaiah said. That's our promise. No more stains that need to be hidden.

Talk to God, let Him clean the stains, and protect that new white shirt.

Connection and Conversation

Here's another confession: My feet are disgusting. I cringe at the thought of anyone seeing them, so just forget about someone touching them. But in biblical times, having your feet washed was a necessary task. They traveled on dirt roads in sandals and bare feet, so they needed attention before walking around inside someone's home. Now let's be honest. Nobody would want the task of washing dirty feet all the time, so this would have been reserved for the servants of the home. Except for one time we're told about in John 13:1–17.

Read through the passage of Jesus washing His disciples' feet. Now take a minute and close your eyes. Imagine what it would be like to have Jesus kneeling in front of you and washing your feet.

What are all your senses experiencing? Are there smells and sounds that you notice?

What are you feeling? Is it uncomfortable or embarrassing?

What are you thinking? Are you fighting the urge to take your feet away and put them back in your shoes?

As I imagine Jesus washing my crusty feet, I feel instantly uncomfortable. It isn't the same embarrassment I feel when I get a pedicure and wonder what the woman is thinking about my filthy feet. It is something deeper. He doesn't belong at my feet. But as I look down and He looks up, our eyes meet.

My first thought is, *I'm not worthy.*

Without missing a moment, I hear Jesus respond. He says, "No, but you're worth it."

Imagine now what it would be like to stand at His feet nailed to the cross. Looking up as He looks down. The positions are reversed, but the exchange the same.

"Am I worthy?"

"No, but you're worth it."

Jesus died while we were all still sinners. All of us.

More important, He conquered the grave while we were all still sinners. All of us.

> For by grace you have been saved through faith.
> And this is not your own doing; it is the gift of God,
> not a result of works, so that no one may boast.
> (Ephesians 2:8–9 NIV)

You were never expected to be worthy of the grace Jesus offers. If that were the case, none of us would meet the requirements. But you have to understand that He considers you worth every moment of ridicule and pain He endured on the cross. Even if you've really messed up.

So lock eyes with the Savior who loves you enough to wash your feet and cleanse your soul. Stop trying to be worthy, and choose to simply live like you're worth it.

HAVE YOU EVER HEARD
OF PUPPY LOVE?

We recently got a puppy. We have other pets, but this is our first puppy, and there is something exceptionally different about the experience.

My kids didn't know I arranged to go meet this little puppy until we were basically on our way there. They were hesitant at first, unsure if this was a gift they could call their own, or if they might just get a few snuggles and then go home empty-handed.

But as we drove home with our fur baby, they excitedly dreamed of life with the new addition to our family. We also talked about some of their new responsibilities, like puppy play and potty breaks. When you're a puppy owner, there are new tasks woven into your daily life, and your focus quickly shifts away from what you did before.

Waking up that next morning, snuggling this little bundle of joy, and thinking about how she had changed our lives in an instant, I thought about God's grace. God had a plan for grace long before we ever knew about it. Before we were even formed. He made the arrangements and sent His Son into this world in human form so we could be saved and become like Him. With His sacrifice on the cross and a willingness to lay down His life on our behalf to overcome sin, He gave us grace. A gift we never even knew to ask for, but one that He loved us enough to offer.

My kids didn't have to earn a puppy; they didn't even know it was a possibility. Just like we don't have to earn grace. It is offered to each of us simply because we are loved and chosen by the One who created us.

If we're honest, though, grace is kind of hard to understand. We approach it cautiously, unsure of what it means or if it's even really something for us. It often seems too good to be true when we think of all the reasons we don't deserve this exceptional gift.

But God is saying, "This gift is for you! Take it and enjoy!"

Then, just like my kids with their puppy, there are changes that take place once we pull that grace into our hearts. Grace shifts our focuses, and we live transformed, loving others in new ways and resisting former patterns of temptation. Developing new thoughts and leaving old speech behind. Spending more time in worship and less in whining.

Grace empowers us to live this new life. Because of our love for Christ and through the grace we have received, it doesn't feel like a chore. It feels like an exciting privilege. Suddenly, we can't imagine life without it, wondering how we existed before this new joy and love entered our lives.

If you haven't already experienced it, I'll be praying that you open your heart to the gift of puppy grace. That you accept Him into your heart and allow the transformation of your life to take over in ways you never could have imagined.

EPIPHANY EPILOGUE

Do Dinosaurs Go to Heaven?

My kids ask some of the craziest questions. As they are learning about the Bible, they aren't afraid to wonder about what they read and hear. As they experience the world around them, they aren't afraid to ponder how things don't always make sense. I always learn a lot when I'm praying and reading to help them figure out an answer.

So why don't I ask more questions? There's a lot that I often wonder about as I read the Bible and as I just figure out how to live in this world as someone who loves Jesus but doesn't quite understand how and why everything is the way it is. Between social issues in the world around me and personal struggles within my own family, the questions can start to pile up. Then I start reading scripture. And to be honest, it sometimes becomes even more confusing.

But is it okay to ask questions? Is it okay to doubt and discuss our issues with God? Yes!

There was this prophet, Habakkuk. He started talking to God, asking questions on behalf of the Israelites. They were struggling. He started questioning God because he saw all of this injustice and evil around them, and nothing made sense.

Does that feel familiar?

God and Habakkuk went back and forth in their conversation. Their discussion was honest and raw. Habakkuk wasn't afraid to tell God how he felt or to ask the tough questions. God responded with honesty, even though it didn't necessarily lead to total clarity. It would be nice to say that there was a clear resolve and definitive answers to the questions raised, but there really wasn't. There were still issues, life still had problems, and questions remained unanswered. But Habakkuk realized that even though he doesn't understand much about God's actions and plans, the conversation helped him to have an unwavering trust in who God is. He chose to rejoice amid his still unanswered questions.

Habakkuk shows us that the point of asking questions isn't always about getting clear answers. It's also about the conversation. It's about the back and forth with God. It's about the open relationship that allows for honest conversations. We learn how to trust God and understand His heart when we ask questions and pay attention to the Word spoken back to us. Like Habakkuk, we begin to find ways to rejoice in the chaos. We start to understand who God is and see Him in the world around us more clearly.

Ask the questions. Read the Bible. Talk to God. Have an epiphany.

Then be prepared to meet Him. Write your own stories about how He has showed up in your life. Share what it means to really know Him. Tell everyone you can about the Creator, Healer, Guide, Provider, Comforter, and Savior who has changed your every day into an eternity.

ABOUT THE AUTHOR

Emily Hill is a hospice chaplain and licensed social worker. She is a graduate of Wesley Seminary and has spent more than a decade in professional ministry serving through a variety of roles. Recent years have led her to meeting God in the many moments of life and she would love for you to join her in the journey.

Printed in the United States
by Baker & Taylor Publisher Services